BOOZE, BROADS AND BAILBONDS

Donna Leslie

This is a fictional novella based loosely on my father's life. The characters, incidents, and dialogue are drawn from the author's imagination and are not to be construed as real. Any resemblance to actual events or persons, living or dead, is entirely coincidental.

First Edition

ISBN: 978-1-09838-195-2

TABLE OF CONTENTS

FOREWORD

My wife of thirty years is always throwing out tidbits about her Dad. He was certainly an interesting person of many talents. She discussed her Dad and his various "connections" and "jobs". They're always fascinating. She keeps saying she should write a book and I keep saying, "Yes, DO write a book".

Due to the Covid-19 quarantine, she's finally done just that. She's done an incredible job of including many details of his life in this book. She always said he was born too late to be the mobster he wanted. I think he was born at the perfect time to be the connected manipulator and casino operator he was born to be. Enjoy this quick read with your favorite drink in your favorite chair. I think she has awakened a new talent and I'm now waiting for book number two.

ACKNOWLEDGEMENT

A special thank you to my husband who encouraged me to continue even when I was tempted to give up. His faith in my effort far exceeded my own.

Thanks to my editor and fellow author, Robert Nathan Stonehill, who patiently guided me through the editorial process.

PROLOGUE

The Albert Pick Motel

We affectionately referred to the Albert Pick Motel as The Pick. In 1954, The Pick was far swankier than most for its time. It stretched over four acres and offered a zoned area for adults-only, as well as families. They had an adults-only restaurant, bar, swimming pool and hot tub. The family-friendly area of the motel offered a buffet resplendent with child-friendly fare. There was an arcade featuring games for the kiddies as well as a movie room for showing films.

There were three conference rooms, the largest capable of seating one hundred. The small conference room was dubbed "the private dining room" and was perpetually reserved for *us*. This is where we gathered to make policy and determine the future of Terre Haute, Indiana, named "Sin City" by the Saturday Evening Post. You don't get a seat at this table unless you are connected. *I was connected.*

I had worked hard to earn my seat at the table. I had spent the last seven years since my divorce from the girls' mother, lovable wife number three, working my way up the food chain to become one of the top dogs. I ran the illegal gambling in Terre Haute; some directly, some indirectly. There was not a political decision made in Terre Haute without my input, and I enjoyed all the benefits of someone who knew how to get things done without violence. I exceled in keeping Terre Haute below the radar until the Saturday Evening Post published their scathing article about "Sin City". That was the beginning of the end.

As I sat in the nearly deserted bar of the Pick, I attempted to rethink the last seven years. I was beginning to doubt my intuition about people. It was definitely time to regroup, maybe start over. It wouldn't be the first time I've had to restart my life. If there is one thing I've learned it's that persistence is everything.

Chapter 1

The End of an Era

The five top dogs in our group met for a quiet dinner at The Pick. It was a farewell party of sorts. Now that Pete Johnson was our official mayor, we needed to discuss what this would mean to our businesses. I could tell from the vehicles in the parking lot, the Judge, Sheriff, and Prosecutor had already arrived.

"Don, how you doin' tonight; your usual? Eleanor! Dry martini for Don and I'll have a whiskey sour," Rob Wiseman said and grabbed a seat next to mine. Judge Stevens and Sheriff John Wesley ordered another round for themselves.

"How about something to eat?" Eleanor dropped the drinks off, and everyone ordered their dinners.

The Judge launched into one of his more interesting hearings from the week. The police chief's girlfriend was arraigned for having attacked the nearly new Lincoln Continental belonging to the Chief's wife. Seems the Chief was trying to break it off with Destiny who was not taking it well.

"I tried to warn him against getting involved with her," said Stevens. "She's a fiery red-head with a matching temperament and this isn't the first time she's gone ballistic in a relationship. It was just three months ago she was in my court room for stalking an ex-boyfriend."

"What did the crazy bitch do this time?" asked Wesley.

"She took a ball bat to the windshield and the lights, and then started toward the house. The cops arrested her before she got to the house, but it shook up Karen pretty badly."

"I'd like to hear the Chief explain that one to Karen."

"He's got a velvet tongue. He'll give her some bullshit story about being targeted for some case he's working on, and she'll buy every word of it," I said. He always finds a way to lie his way out.

Food arrived and conversation dwindled. An hour later, dishes were cleared and second and third rounds of drinks were delivered. Eleanor picked up her tip, and secured the room.

"These weren't local guys, Don. I'm thinking Indianapolis or Chicago. They were definitely feds. I only caught bits and pieces, but I distinctly heard them mention the Reservation by name." John Wesley confided.

"Thanks for the info, John. Your honor, I don't have any reason to be concerned do I? We're square with everyone, right," I asked.

"You're good, Don. Everything is handled," replied Stevens. "You don't have anything to worry about."

That proved to be a load of shit! Two days later I got a visit from the FBI.

****

Thanks to the unique location of the Reservation, I knew immediately when they turned into the long drive. “Ladies and gentlemen we are about to receive a visit from the FBI. Continue to enjoy your dinner and a complimentary cocktail. They are not interested in anything in this building. Relax and enjoy”.

Mickey and her staff quickly dispersed the cocktails and I went out to meet our visitors. Even without their badges, they were recognizable. The three black Crown Vics were followed by a seventeen foot Ryder truck. I met them in the driveway.

“Mr. Leslie?”

I nodded.

“I’m field agent, Dick Henning from the FBI, and we have a warrant to search the premises. This is Pete Drummer and Mark Titus.” The rest of the band of merry men evidently didn’t warrant an introduction.

"If you don't mind, I have guests for dinner in the restaurant. What you want is in the barn." I confessed. The caravan followed me as I walked down the path toward the barn with the Ryder truck close behind.

"Gentlemen, I believe this is what you were looking for." I stood there proud of the professional appearance of the old barn. It was Vegas in miniature. "Why don't we step into the office?"

Dick Henning and his two seconds in command followed me upstairs to the office. As functional as the casino floor was, the office was pure elegance. A red leather, tufted sofa and two navy wing back chairs faced a large, ornately carved mahogany desk. There were bookcases covering one entire wall, and a large floor safe. I motioned to Dick and his henchmen to have a seat.

"Gentlemen, I think there must be some mistake here," I started. "I believe I am current on my tax payments and I'm at a loss as to why you might have a warrant to search anything. Would you like to elaborate?" I asked, knowing full well that all the necessary palms had been greased at great expense.

"Mr. Leslie, I don't know what you are eluding to, but our warrant is quite clear. Locate and confiscate all illegal gambling equipment found on these premises." Dick was certainly turning out to be a dick. He handed me the warrant.

I was starting to get more than a little pissed at these fuckers. "This is signed by Judge Stevens. Now I know this is a mistake. Let me give the judge a call." I said as I picked up my phone to call. The judge didn't answer his private number, and I had to leave a message. Now I was really starting to boil. You'd think twenty thousand dollars would buy you better treatment.

"Sorry, Mr. Leslie, we need to load up your equipment. We'll also need any bookkeeping records you have on the premises." Dick-face commanded.

"I don't keep bookkeeping records you prick", I said. Dick went down to supervise the gathering of equipment as the two henchmen rifled through the bookcase and desk. I poured a cognac, lit a Lucky Strike and settled on the couch to watch the Bobbsey twins search the office. When prompted, I opened the safe which revealed less than five thousand dollars and no paperwork. *How stupid do you think I am, you gutless wonders?*

I took a long draw off my Lucky and reflected on how business used to be. You could trust the fuckers you paid off then. Just as I was ruminating about the state of my donations, the phone rang. It was the Judge.

"Don, did you call me? Sorry, I was in the middle of something," he said.

"I've got a problem here. I have a driveway full of FBI agents with a very large Ryder truck who are insistent about hauling off my equipment. They have a warrant signed by you. Would you like to explain that to me?" I asked.

"Shit. Let me talk to the agent in charge," he said.

"Hey, Dick, you have a phone call up here." I emphasized the Dick.

Dick crawled up the steps and took the phone from my hand. "This is agent Henning." There was a very long pause on this end of the call that ended with "yes sir, I understand. Sorry for the inconvenience." Henning apologized. "All right guys, back to the cars. Mr. Leslie, there seems to have been some kind of clerical error. I apologize for the inconvenience. We'll be on our way. Fellows, get back to the cars. Leave everything," he yelled down the stairs. Everyone looked thoroughly confused, but got in the cars and they were all gone in ten minutes.

I sat on the couch sipping my cognac wondering what the hell just happened. The phone rang and it was the Judge. "Don, meet me at The Pick. I don't want to discuss this on the phone. See you in fifteen minutes?" he asked.

"Sure. See you there," I replied.

When I pulled the Caddie into the parking lot, the Judge was already there. My martini was waiting and the dining room was empty, with the exception of the Judge.

"What the hell just happened?" I asked.

"I'm sorry. That whole thing was supposed to go down tomorrow, but Dick jumped the gun on me. I got tied up in that God damn meeting with our new mayor, and didn't get you called earlier today. I apologize again" said Stevens.

"Just tell me what the hell is going on," I said, still irritated at the whole escapade.

"Our new Mayor has brought the Feds in to do a full court press in Terre Haute, and they were starting with you. Seems that little prick has started to believe his own propaganda, and is intent upon cleaning up the city as fast as possible. I got backed into a corner and had to sign the warrant, but they were supposed to arrive tomorrow to find nothing. Fucking over-anxious little jerk." The Judge seemed as upset as I was.

"So now what happens?" I asked.

"Empty the barn because they will be back tomorrow. I can't stop that, but if there's nothing to find it will just be another exercise. Can you get it emptied before tomorrow?" the Judge asked.

"Sure, let me make a phone call," I called Ronnie, my right hand man. "Ron, I need to get everything out of the barn and stashed somewhere that can't be tied back to me. Can you get some guys and get this done? Yeah, tonight. We're going to have visitors tomorrow. Thanks." I turned back to the Judge. "He'll get it done. We'll be clean by tomorrow."

We finished our meal and Judge Stevens left early to go home. I moved to the bar and selected a table nestled in a corner far away from the tourists. I sat there nursing my martini, puffing on my Lucky Strike and contemplating the last fifteen years. It occurred to me that maybe I wasn't as intuitive about people as I had assumed. I was at the top of the heap, living the good life, and a man of importance. What happened?

Chapter 2

A Little Background

People have horror stories about their childhood they love to share. *I don't.* I was a spoiled child. My family had nearly nothing, but what we had was split between my mother and me. Dad ran away from his childhood home when he was eleven and worked as a coal miner in Kentucky and Southern Indiana for most of his life. He relocated to Terre Haute in his forties. There he met Mother, twenty years his junior, who was enrolled at Indiana State Teachers College hoping one day to teach elementary education.

Dad absolutely doted on her. Although she was one of six children, she was what they called then a "change of life baby". There was an eight year gap between her next youngest sibling and her.

She was afforded all the perks of being the last in the lineage. Mom had many tactics to keep Dad conforming to what she wanted. Like a two-year-old she would throw tantrums, cry remarkably real tears, or when all else failed, threaten to end it all.

Isaac "Shorty" Leslie

My Dad, "Shorty" as he was nicknamed, lavished Mom with anything she wanted. Even during their early marriage at the height of the depression, my Dad worked hauling ashes out of basement furnaces for extra money when others were lamenting there was no work available. We never suffered as others did. Thanks to my Mom's sewing skills, and Dad's work ethics, my Mom always looked like a fashion plate.

My Mom, Beatrice Leslie

When I came home from the Great War, I did as so many others did. I found a girl, married and had two beautiful daughters. We had barely been married a year when my Dad, who was working as a night janitor at the courthouse in Terre Haute, was found dead. He suffered from black lung disease from years of working the mines, and they speculated he became short of breath, sat down and simply died. Mom had never written a check, had no idea of their circumstances, and had no intention of learning. She moved in with us. When the children came along, she was the built-in babysitter.

Since Mom was now watching the girls, my wife got a job selling new cars at Jack Thrasher Ford. I made guest appearances when I wasn't on the road, which was constantly. I became the star salesman for Campbell's Soup. In those days, salesmen made the rounds selling various products to grocery stores. There were other products, but Campbell's Soup was the cornerstone of the company. Our garage remained unused by the car because it was filled with cases of soup and boxes of advertising items.

Periodically I'd have to rescue one of the Campbell Kid life-sized cardboard advertising boards from their rooms. They delighted in having tea with the Campbell Kids, although they were told numerous times they were not toys.

We led separate lives under the same roof. Mom took care of the basics. My wife worked at Jack Thrasher Ford where she met husband number two. I screwed around with whomever I pleased, and we all occasionally showed up at the same time at the house. When the kids were seven and five, we divorced.

The divorce was a catalyst for change in career as well. I made up my mind after traveling the roads over the tristate area there had to be a better way to finance the lifestyle I craved. As long as I was working for someone else, I was never going to do anything but eke out a mediocre living. I knew I could sell anything to anybody. Insurance appeared to have the least investment with the best return, so I pored over the regulations and aced my test, getting my insurance license on the first sitting.

At its height, there were eighty-one houses and four hundred and eighty five prostitutes operating in the "red light district", but as politics changed and the college usurped more of the district, the number of houses shrank. There were still adequate facilities to service the locals and occasional college students. Because of the neighborhood, I got a helluva deal on a little house which I converted into my office. I started the Vigo Insurance Agency on North 13th Street in 1951. Within three months, I had sold enough insurance to qualify for the $100,000 club. I was rewarded with a gold cigarette case with a $100,000 written in small diamonds on the front. The insurance proved to be a good basic income, but certainly wasn't going to support the lifestyle I envisioned for myself.

I met a lot of people in Terre Haute while selling life insurance including a very likeable fellow named Gerald Meeks. He was a great mechanic and worked on my Mom's Dodge several times. Her diabetes affected her eyesight causing her to misjudge distances. Usually this involved hitting inanimate objects, and occasionally a parked car as well. I suspect moving vehicles were able to avoid her, but stationary objects couldn't escape. Since Mom's car needed frequent repairs, I got to know Gerald pretty well.

One day he approached me with an interesting business proposition. He could take cars we bought at the auction, spruce up the cars, "turn back the mileage", and then sell them as nearly new! He needed a little start-up money to get going which I was glad to provide for half-interest in the business. I lined up a sympathetic loan officer at the Terre Haute National Bank who was willing to finance our buyers, and arranged for a substantial building with two repair bays and an office. City Motors was born!

I had no idea when we started City Motors it would lead to my first brush with law enforcement. We started small and kept building with more salesmen, then more locations. Soon we had a network covering the entire southern third of Indiana. Staff continued to grow and I passed on the day-to-day operations to the new president of

City Motors, Raymond Stock. I became more of a silent partner---very silent. Ultimately, people got a little too comfortable and a little too sloppy. That culminated with the arrest of sixteen individuals, including the president of City Motors, Raymond Stock, and the head of the installment loan division of the Terre Haute National Bank, Samuel Taylor. The president received fifty-four months and the banker got fifty-two months. Five of those arrested received probation. I was one of those lucky individuals who received probation as was Gerald-thanks to a great lawyer and a *special* relationship with the judge.

When the final audit was done, $334,000 had vanished without a trace. I had gifted myself with a nice little nest egg from *that* adventure, and managed to get out with a slap on the wrist, so it was time to find another project.

I always did my best thinking during an afternoon of golf at the Elks, and Mayor Roy Drucker, my golfing buddy, was always up for an afternoon away from the office.

I called Roy on his private line. "Roy, how about a refreshing afternoon. Are you game? Great meet you at the Elks." Periodically, it was necessary for our mental health to have a 'refreshing afternoon' as we called it. That entailed eighteen holes, followed by a couple drinks at the nineteenth hole, and then dinner at the Elks Club. This wasn't time spent plotting our next political move. Quite the contrary. Roy was the only person I truly counted as a friend. We both had a need to step away from playing the game occasionally, and share relaxing activities; there was no ulterior motive. It was just two guys relaxing.

"I'm glad you called Don. I was in need of some down time. How's your Mom doing?" Roy asked.

"Great. She's so happy to have a new house, and the girls come over for a month each summer. She really looks forward to that," I said. "How about your wife, how's Sarah?"

"Wonderful. She's really a homebody. She loves spending time with Mary, playing board games. Scrabble is her favorite. Mary takes care of the housework, and Sarah is free to shop or hang out with her girlfriends. Luncheons at the Goodie Shop are one of their favorite hangouts," Roy explained.

We changed our shoes in the clubhouse, picked up the golf cart, and headed for the first tee. The day was perfect for golf. The sun was out, temperature a nice balmy seventy, and the course was immaculate. That was one of the things I appreciated about the Elks. Their golf course was top notch. They had a pro who insisted things be as perfect as possible, unusual for a small club like ours. The Elks also had a wonderful swimming pool, and I would bring Mom and the girls out for a day at the Elks. They could swim, eat, and indulge in doing nothing while putting it all on the tab. The girls liked the idea they only had to say 'charge to Daddy, please'.

"Beautiful shot, Roy." I watched his tee shot sail within thirty feet of the green.

"Thanks. If I could putt, I'd have a decent average. See if you can top that shot, Don."

"I'm pretty rusty. It's been too long since we've been out here, but I'll give it a shot," I complained as I stepped up to the tee. My average hovers around 75-80 which isn't bad for a duffer, but it's certainly nothing to brag about. Roy's average was more in the 90 range. My tee shot felt great; form was good, felt relaxed and fluid. Too bad, that didn't show in the shot itself. My ball ended just inside the rough about forty feet from the tee.

"Well that looked like it was going to be a great shot; great form, Don. Someone forgot to tell the ball, though," Roy teased.

"Yeah, like they say....the surgery was a success, but the patient died," I said as we climbed into the cart and headed for my ball.

We spent the afternoon with varying amounts of success, and ended our eighteen holes with Roy shooting a reasonable 98 and my game was really off at 89. Regardless, it was a great afternoon, and put us both in a relaxed state.

Back at the clubhouse, Roy ordered us both drinks as we retold our greatest and worst shots to each other as though we hadn't just witnessed them for ourselves.

"I think I'm ready for a nice big, fat steak. What do you say, Don. Shall we adjourn to the dining room?" asked Roy.

"I'm ready," I said. Locally, the club had the best surf and turf available. There was a restaurant in Paris, IL that I sometimes went to that was extraordinary, but the club was a great second choice and far more convenient.

Eventually the conversation turned to work. "So what's your next great adventure, Don?" Roy asked between bites.

"I haven't decided. Have you got suggestions?" I asked Roy.

"There is a guy from Brazil, Indiana, who comes over and writes bonds on certain days, but he is an older guy and ready to hang it up. Since you already have a working relationship with the sheriff and judge, I could see you taking over the bail bond business," Roy suggested.

"You might have an idea there. I'll check out what kind of revenue that could produce. It could be a good addition to the insurance business," I said.

When a judge sets bail at $100,000, the suspect doesn't have to pay $100,000. A third person, a bail bondsman, guarantees the suspect will appear for his future arraignments. For the privilege of guaranteeing the appearance, the suspect must pay the bondsman ten percent of the bond amount. So a $100,000 bail would cost the suspect $10,000. If the suspect decides to skip bail, the court will expect the full amount of the bail money to be surrendered to the court as punishment for doing a piss poor job of babysitting the suspect. The court will give you a date for producing the suspect. The bondsman has to chase down the bail jumper or if the suspect is extremely dangerous he can hire a bounty hunter. I enjoyed chasing down the occasional jumper. There were only three times I had to leave the state to retrieve a jumper, and I never had to use my gun on any of them. Once found, they gave up peacefully and we returned to the Terre Haute jail. It's a lot like gambling. You're betting you can hunt down the skipper before the assigned date, or it's going to cost you a shit load of money.

After checking out the possible income from the bail bonds, I decided Roy had a great idea. When the scandal of the City Motors died off, I opened the Vigo Bonding Agency. After I helped Judge Stevens get elected, I developed a virtual monopoly as the ONLY bail bondsman in Terre Haute. Despite the efforts of the Indianapolis-based bonding companies, they were repeatedly unable to make headway.

Chapter 3

Bonding Out

Left to Right: Jules Horwick, Irwin Gordon and Leo Shaffer being led from the federal building in Terre Haute Image from "Big, Big Bettors Hide, Hide and Hide" - Life, September 1st, 1958 edition

It was a lucky break for me when "the largest bookie operation outside Las Vegas" opened their shop on the second floor of the old Hansen Building at 671 Wabash Avenue. When they were busted by the U.S. Treasury Department, it made headlines and made me the go-to guy to spring them. The group arrested included Sammy "The Slammer" Cook and Joey Johnson from Chicago, Irwin Gordon and Tony Colotta from Las Vegas, and Leo Shaffer and Jules Horwick from Indianapolis. I offered my services to all of them, but the Indianapolis guys bonded out with a guy from Indy. The Chicago guys contacted their folks in Chicago, but the Vegas guys signed on with me. It doesn't hurt to have a few Vegas guys *owe you.* Everybody got off free and clear except for Sammy. He must have made some kind of deal with the Chicago group, but he got five years. I admit I actually enjoyed that. He was a bit of a prick with an attitude.

Tony Colotta was the boss of the Terre Haute operation and embodied everything you'd expect from a Las Vegas mobster. He was thirty or thirty-five years old and had jet-black, curly hair with stunning, electric- blue eyes. He dressed well and had a gold pinky ring on his right hand with a large emerald. On his left wrist he wore a heavy gold bracelet. He and I hit it off right away.

I spent a lot of time with Tony while awaiting his trial. Fortunately for me, when he learned I was a frequent Vegas visitor, we spent a lot of that time hanging out in Vegas. Tony owned the Flamingo Hotel and Casino, and I was able to take full advantage of complimentary stays. I learned a lot from following Tony around the Flamingo as he worked the floor.

"How are you ladies doing tonight? Are you stealing all my money?" he asked the group of three senior ladies parked in front of their respective slot machines. They glowed when he singled them out. I took note.

We walked on through the casino. "How do you give everyone the individual attention they need," I asked.

"You can't give everyone your full attention. The trick is to make what little attention you give them seem unique and special to them. We have trained individuals who work exclusively with our whales (high rollers). I still make an appearance in the high roller areas but that is to assure them I am supervising the people helping them. I always personally introduce their contact person as soon as they arrive. I also make sure that I check in on them. My people are trained to notify me if they feel a personal visit would be helpful and I never question their wisdom. Of course, if there is a problem, they would call me immediately," he explained.

We left the casino floor and started making the rounds of the high roller rooms. Tony immediately checked in with his staff upon arrival in the poker room.

"What do I need to know, Linda? He asked.

"At table one Mr. Anderson is ahead by $30,000-$35,000; about half of that came from Mr. Norton. Table two is relatively equally distributed. No big winner or loser there," Linda replied.

"Thanks Linda." Tony headed off to table one. When there was a break in the action he approached the table. "Gentlemen, how are things going? Linda taking good care of you?"

"I was going to call you. My shower is draining poorly so I end up standing in two inches of water," complained Mr. Norton.

"I'm sorry to hear that. I can take care of that immediately," Tony said. "It will be fixed before you return to your room. Is there anything else I can do for you gentlemen?" There were no further complaints from the group. The waitress arrived with fresh drinks for everyone as we were leaving.

Mr. Norton could have easily called maintenance to repair the shower, but chose to make a point of going to the top with his complaint. As soon as we cleared the area, Tony got on his walkie-talkie to the front desk. "We have an unhappy guest. Mr. Norton has a shower that is draining slowly. Please have someone up there immediately."

"Yes sir, Tony. We'll get it handled right away," replied a chipper female voice.

Tony was a chameleon. His demeanor changed based on who he was addressing. "You have a comfortable, friendly approach with the general casino population, but I noticed you shifted to a more formal approach with the whales. It's almost like you're their personal assistant. Mr. Norton could have easily called the front desk, but he asked you to handle it," I said.

"Mr. Norton is losing, not a lot, but losing just the same. He doesn't like losing. It made him feel better to ask me to handle a menial task for him," explained Tony. "It took me two minutes, and it made him feel more important; a win for both of us. Every person reacts differently, and you have to understand their motivation before you can control any situation. It's all about perception. I could have told him to call maintenance, but it was important to him for me to accept the responsibility of catering to his needs."

"What if one of the blue hairs had asked the same thing when you talked to them?" I asked.

"I would have done the same thing, but I would have called the front desk in front of them and teased them about not letting their beautiful little feet stand in water," replied Tony. "Know your audience and then you know how to play to them. People let their ego get in the way of what they want to accomplish. I've worked hard to get where I am, and I could have copped an attitude and told either group to call maintenance, but both of them will remember that I personally addressed their needs. I've created a positive encounter and all it took was a call on the walkie-talkie."

"I get it. Thanks." I continued to shadow Tony throughout the night and many other nights as we awaited the outcome of his trial. I think he enjoyed being the teacher to his latest recruit. He was a master manipulator and I was eager to learn all I could.

"You know Don, you're a bright guy and you've done a good job with both of your businesses, but the real money lies in gambling. You really should think about adding that to your business. You already have most of the connections you need," Tony told me on one of our walkabouts.

"I'm not sure how a casino would work in Terre Haute," I said.

"You don't have to have a full-fledged casino to make money at gambling. Pick a specialty. There are plenty of ways to make money on a smaller scale." Tony suggested.

"I'll give it some serious thought, Tony. Thanks for the idea." The bonding business was getting pretty routine although it was still a good money maker, but I did need a little something else to do. There were ample back room poker parlors in Terre Haute, and bookie operations were obviously not a good bet. After considering various options, I decided on a Keno game. I started searching for an appropriate venue for a weekly keno game. Within a month, I had rented the Red Man Hall.

Chapter 4

Taking a Gamble

The Red Man Hall, formerly a Jewish Temple.

The Improved Order of Red Man was a fraternal organization for white-men only, based on Native American rituals. At its height in 1935, they had half a million members in the U.S.! Now the remnants of the group gathered for their very secretive rites in the upper floors of the building. The building currently used as their home base had been a Jewish Temple in its former life, and though it lacked the splendor it once had, there were vestiges of its former glory. I was told the upstairs was fabulous, but the only proof I had was the very ornate stairway and the stage in fellowship hall. The stairway was golden oak and was massive in scale. Each spindle was individually carved and had a diameter of a little over three and a half inches. The banister curved around at the bottom and laid atop a newel post covered with what appeared to be angel-like beings frolicking in a garden. I was sure the newel post had to weigh two hundred pounds. The other vestige from the temple was the framework surrounding the stage in fellowship hall. There was a large medallion shaped crest centered on the top of the stage from which all the carvings grew. They covered the top third of the stage opening. It was an impressive sight. I always wanted to take a look upstairs at the untouched areas, but was never able to accomplish that.

The Red Man were more than happy to have a little bonus income as their membership dwindled. I was delighted to have found such a huge hall, and they provided all the tables and chairs as well. I hired checkers to take the money, kitchen staff, and we were set for our first game. We held the games on Tuesday evening 7-10, and on opening night we had a full house! It was a surprisingly mixed crowd. Of course there were the veteran gamblers happy to have a source of gaming close to home.

The real bread and butter of the Keno game were the older people that frequented the charitable bingo games held at St. Andrews Catholic Church. They were quick to switch their allegiance, preferring the real money offered by the Keno game rather than the household cleaners and toilet paper offered by the church.

Despite many discussions on why she could not play at my games, my Mother would sneak in anyway. Stationing herself in the smaller room in the back, she would hope I wouldn't recognize her voice when she won. I pretended not to notice and she tried to act inconspicuous. Her track record turned out to be exceedingly poor, winning only rarely, so it was really more of a game we played than a serious problem.

"Don, we don't have a sound system." Ronnie mentioned half an hour before opening.

"Shit, I forgot all about that. I'll make do." There had been a lot of details, as well as an unending number of donations to be made to get this off the ground, and I had forgotten about the sound system.

I sat behind the ball machine and we started up. “Our first game is straight Keno, five in a row. Scream out when you have all five and one of the checkers will come to verify your card. First game is worth $500 to the winner. We’ll have a $1000 coverall at the end of the night, folks, so stay with us.” No one has ever complained they couldn’t hear me, and Ronnie stationed in the back of the second room, gave me the signal that tonight would be no exception.

“Our first ball, K10.”

Tony was right, the money came rolling in every week. The insurance agency became an afterthought as the bail bonds and keno game brought in the big bucks. A lovely blue-haired matron yelled “Bingo” with great enthusiasm. “Ladies and gentlemen please hold your cards until we have verified the win,” I bellowed. She became a regular and one of my very favorite people. She dressed with a total disregard for her age, preferring instead colorful, flowered shawls and large, chunky jewelry. No one would ever accuse her of blending in.

Like my Mother, she had a son that worried over her gambling habit. She would occasionally spend the rent money gambling, so I would get a call from her irate son. I'd refund the rent money to her son, and promise to not allow her into the games again. About four times a year we'd have a rent crisis. Each time I would feign ignorance as to how she could have escaped our detection, the rent would be returned to her son, and she would enjoy another three months of uninterrupted play. It was a dance we would continue until her death at ninety-six.

The checker picked up the suspected card and read the numbers back to me. "B10." "Yeah". I replied. "I23." "Yeah." "N27". "Yeah." "G38." "Yeah." And "O49." "Ladies and gentlemen we have a winner. That's our first win tonight for $500. Checker please pay the lady. Thank you," I said. "Clear your cards for our next game."

After six months or so, I decided it was time to expand the business. Certainly, I wouldn't be able to do so in the city, but I acquired a farm just outside Terre Haute. It had a small, five-room house and a large red barn. There was only a gravel road leading from the main highway down into the valley where the property was located.

Front of Menu from Reservation

I turned the house into an intimate restaurant. The kitchen and storage needs took up the back two rooms. The front two rooms had five four-top tables in each. The larger room also held a small walk-up bar. The sunroom had a player piano surrounded by a custom counter with stools. The wives continued drinking at the piano bar while the husbands retired to the barn. The player piano played old favorites, suitable for singing along, which became much more enthusiastic as the drinks flowed.

Occasionally one of the wives would take a turn at actually playing the piano, with hilarious results.

Tony provided me up with the needed equipment to set up the barn as a real casino. It had all the requisite gambling devices, in fewer quantity. The barn was red as barns should be and had a large plaque across the doorway with an Indian chieftain and the "Reservation" lit with light bulbs reminiscent of the old Vegas signs, a touch that cost more than anticipated but worth every penny. The green velvet of the craps, roulette and black jack tables had that familiar look. There were three slot machines; battling space ships began shooting their lasers, Elvis started gyrating to Blue Suede shoes, and Aqua Man made underwater sounds. Two poker tables sat on one end of the barn and a ten foot long bar stretched the length of the barn to the slot machines at the other end, directly across from the large double barn doors. The large mirror behind the bar reflected all the booze bottles and made them sparkle in the bright lights.

Our first night we invited fifteen business associates and their wives. Dinner was on me, and there was a cash bar. We had three judges, the sheriff, prosecutor, chief of police, fire chief, and several of my favorite attorneys and cops. We did no advertising since this was a private club. It provided another revenue stream, but more importantly, it was an easy way to keep in touch with all of my contacts.

Chapter 5

The Players

There were basically five individuals, including myself that ran Terre Haute. There was Judge Stevens, Prosecutor Robert Wiseman, Sheriff John Wesley, Mayor Roy Drucker and me. The Chief of Police was well-paid, but just a glorified errand boy. You know the old joke, buy three politicians; get one free.

Judge Jeffrey Stevens' family had been part of the political scene in Terre Haute as long as I can remember. His father and grandfather were both federal judges, and the family assumed Jeffrey would follow in their footsteps. He got involved with drugs in his sophomore year of college, but with a stint in a luxurious Wyoming rehab center and a very special roommate selected by daddy, he was able to kick the habit and finish college with honors. He went on to I.U. Law School, with roommate in tow, and passed the bar on his first attempt.

Sheriff John Wesley was a cop who came up through the ranks. He had a lovely wife, three kids and a spacious home in a new subdivision. His four-year stint in the Marines taught him team building skills that helped him create a loyal following, both with the public and within the department. Starting out as an enthusiastic rookie, the badge lost its shine after fifteen years. Putting his skills to use for our mutual benefit earned him a place at the table. He was a total crook and didn't do anything without earning a little stipend for his efforts. I appreciated his straight-forward approach to whatever needed doing. He named the price, and I paid. I always got what I paid for and never had to worry about his loyalty to me, and he did it all while appearing to be Terre Haute's favorite son.

Prosecutor Robert Wiseman was another story. His knowledge of the law was amazing. He could ferret out loop holes or contradictory statues that assured him of whatever outcome he desired. He was dynamic to watch in court and catered to the press so convincingly that they became his greatest supporter. He came from a wealthy family and had virtually no skeletons in his closet. His motive was the sheer joy of toying with others for his own amusement. He was the most challenging of the top dogs. It required extra effort on my part to keep him engaged in the game. If he became bored, he could be a problem. He was also the one I admired the most.

Mayor Roy Drucker was raised in an orphanage. Since he was nearly twelve when his parents were killed in a car crash, he was beyond the age of adoption. No one wanted a twelve year old, so he spent the next six years in the Terre Haute Children's Home. Hard times can make a man out of a boy quickly. Drucker developed a knack for charming people to get what he wanted. At twenty three he was elected mayor of Terre Haute, a job he would hold for 28 consecutive years. He was a kindred spirit. He worked hard and earned everything he got. He appreciated the things money could buy, and didn't limit himself. He enjoyed good food, great booze, beautiful women, golf, poker, and knowing he was respected by the masses. He was probably most like me so it was no surprise I counted him as a friend as well as a colleague.

Then there was me. I am one of those individuals who sets a goal and then beats the hell out of it. I'm a conqueror. I never graduated from college but I never stopped learning. Whenever there is an opportunity, I grab it. Some people find me a little self-centered: I call that confidence. Some would say I'm a bit of a show off: I call that being well-dressed and well-groomed. Some people resent my personal power: I strive for more. I like me.

Judge Stevens was up for reelection and I was in a perfect position to help, but the judge had not always been favorable to the local mobsters. We would need to have a long talk before I signed up to work on the Judge's campaign. I met the Judge at the private dining room at the Albert Pick Motel along with Sheriff John Wesley and City Prosecutor Robert Wiseman, both of whom I had been paying for some time. The Judge knew the sheriff and prosecutor, of course, but we were about to have a totally different type of conversation.

“Glad you could join us, Judge,” I said as I rose to shake his hand. “You know Rob and John.”

“Yes, of course, hi fellas,” he replied shaking hands around the table.

We all ordered lunch and drinks and talked about the weather until the food was served. “Katie, see that we’re not disturbed, please.” I asked.

“Judge, I know you’ve been concerned about the bad press the city has been getting and I’m sure you’re wondering if there is going to be some blowback on your campaign.” I noted. “I think I have a proposition that could help all of us get what we want.”

“I’m listening,” he said.

“Rob, John and I have a relationship that has been working relatively well for all of us. I agree that the level of gambling in the city will be kept at an acceptable level, and they agree to not bother my operation. I don’t need a bunch of blue-haired old ladies being arrested on the evening news. There are some other establishments in our city who have reciprocal agreements as well. It is not in anyone’s best interest to have any kind of violence associated between competing factions. We keep things peaceful and offer entertainment for consenting adults. No one gets hurt and we all come away richer."

"Obviously we have to appear to be hard on crime so there are some sacrificial busts that make the papers," stated John.

"I know the routine," said the Judge.

"Then you know there are already a lot of people, influential people with money, who would like this situation to continue to be profitable for all concerned. The last thing we need is a vigilante Judge making a name for himself.' I stated. "I think you can understand where I'm heading here."

"Unfortunately, these "busts" are sometimes thrown out because of a technicality; an inaccurate warrant, poor timing busting an operation that seems to have vanished, etc. You're a smart guy. You get the picture. It requires a coordinated effort between the offices. Occasionally, some low-level individual will get convicted so it appears your team is doing a fabulous job. It is a careful, well-orchestrated act which keeps the money flowing to all of us," explained Rob.

"I understand perfectly, but it has to appear that I am hard on corruption in the city." insisted the Judge.

"Before I can commit financial support for your campaign, I need to know we can get you on board," I explained. "We need a judge to join the team."

"Your campaign needs a major influx of both money and influence. I know some excellent people who can craft a campaign to elect a monkey. They're expensive but I think we can cover that for you. Do we have an agreement?" I asked.

"Absolutely," said the Judge.

I immediately called my team of experts to start working on Judge Stevens' campaign. True to his word once the election was over, the Judge became a valuable addition to the team.

Everything was going well and then I received a call from the mayor, Roy Drucker.

"Don, we need to talk. Can you meet me at the Pick for dinner tonight?" asked Roy.

"Sure. See you there about 6:30," I replied.

I walked into the dining room at the Pike. There sat Roy all alone and looking quite glum. "You sounded desperate on the phone."

"That God damn article in the Saturday Evening Post has got everybody riled up, and that smug, little prick, Pete Johnson, is going to make a play for my town," he raged. 'That little shit thinks he's going to clean up Terre Haute for the decent folk."

"Roy, calm down. You're going to give yourself a heart attack," I offered. "I can have him handled. Just say the word. I know people who can make him go away."

"It's not just him, Don. Indiana State College is expanding. They've bought up the entire Cherry Street area and are building apartments for their students. They're putting pressure on me to clean things up because parents don't want to spend big bucks to send their kids to a college in "Sin City", Roy complained. "And frankly, I'm tired. Maybe it's time for this old horse to retire from politics; to sit on the porch and watch the other guys make a mess of things."

"Roy, you can't do that. You ARE Terre Haute. People love you." I needed him to stay in office. I had a great deal of money invested in him. Besides, I loved the guy. We were alike in so many ways. We both loved the game; poker, golf or people.

"Why don't you come to Vegas with me and we can relax, blow off a little steam, and rethink our positions. Tony can fix us up in a suite at the Flamingo. We'll think better with the sun in our face and a martini in our hand," I suggested.

"By God Don, that sounds too good to pass up. Let's do it."

"I'll call Tony and set it up. Excuse me a minute." I went to the house phone in the lobby. "Tony, Don Leslie…"

"Like I wouldn't know that voice anywhere."

"I have a problem here. Mayor Drucker is a little down and is talking about not running in the upcoming election. I need him to run and beat Pete Johnson or I'm out of business here." I offered. "I convinced him a weekend in Vegas with me is a perfect way to regroup for the election."

"No problem Don. You get him out here and we'll make sure he comes back loaded with cash and ideas for his win over that little do-gooder," assured Tony. I knew I could count on him. "We'll have a limo at the airport. Call me when you get your flights. See you then."

I went back to the dining room. "Mayor, we need to book airfare to Vegas. When do you want to leave?"

"How about an early bird flight on Friday," Roy suggested.

We left for Vegas the next Friday. Just in time because Roy was making some seriously scary noises about quitting again. We stretched back in first class and enjoyed martinis as we watched the attendants load the regulars onto the plane. Roy wasted no time getting to his favorite subject…defeat.

"I'm telling you, I think there's a rat in my office. The little prick knows every move I make before I make it," he complained. The little prick did have a name. His name was Pete Johnson. That's how he got his nickname. He was barely five foot tall, and we guessed that his johnson matched the size of the rest of his body….hence, the little prick. His height was little; his girth was not. He carried at least an extra 40 pounds, and on a little guy that's a lot. He had a way of inciting a crowd though. His do-gooder "I'm here to protect the citizens of Terre Haute from organized crime" routine was appealing.

"What makes you think you have a rat? What could they possibly be providing to whom?" I asked. The "Tribune" has always had an inside line into the politics in Terre Haute and this was proving to be a challenging election. Of course, they had the goods. That was their business.

"The Post called the entire town apathetic about the criminal presence in Terre Haute. It made even the regular folks look like idiots, or worse, crooks, drunks and thieves. No one is going to like that. If they don't throw me out, it looks like they don't care about their city," Roy said.

"I know you might think that would be the case, but let's just consider this. You could turn this around to your advantage. It's not that Terre Haute is a gangster town, it's that the Post is out to smear Terre Haute because of a long-standing political squabble with the editor of the Post," I supposed.

"What political squabble? Who's the editor at the Post? Roy asked.

"I don't know, and don't care. We can manufacture whatever scandal we want. We just have to show the people a way they can keep their pride and their beloved Mayor. Don't fret. We've got this," I assured Roy. "Another round, please miss."

****

Just as promised Tony had sent a limo to pick us up at the airport. When we pulled up to the

Flamingo. Henry was waiting at the curb. He introduced himself and whisked us up to the executive suite without stopping to check us in. I offered a tip to him. “No sir, Mr. Leslie, your money is no good at the Flamingo. You are Mr. Colotta’s guest. I will be your contact while at the hotel. If there is anything, anything at all you need, just ring #6 to reach me. I’ve arranged for a massage later this afternoon just to get out the kinks from your flight. That’s at two if that fits your schedule. Will that be alright, sir?” Henry asked.

“That is a perfect plan, Henry. Thank you.”

That gave Roy and me just over an hour to unpack. Since it was early afternoon, the neon lights of Vegas weren’t evident yet. We investigated the suite. There were two bedrooms with baths, a living/dining area, and a fully stocked bar suitable for a major party. Like everything in Vegas it was totally overdone.

“Which bedroom you want, Roy?” I asked.

“I’m standing in front of this one so I guess I’ll take it.”

We split to shower, unpack and met at the bar just in time for Henry to reappear. He had in tow, two lovely young ladies in extremely short shorts and tank tops which left little to the imagination. “Gentlemen, this is Candy”, pointing to the brunette beauty to his left, “and this is Laura”, gesturing to the fair skinned blonde to his right. These are your massage therapists,” Henry explained. “While they set up why don’t I show you some of the finer points of the suite?”

“Henry, I think you’ve already shown us the finer points of the suite,” Roy said, flashing a grin at the brunette.

“Mr. Leslie here is the control box for the suite. The drapes are operated thusly. The heavy pink velvet drapes drew slowly around the windows circling the suite. This operates the music and TV with all the adjustments. This second control box is the lighting.” Henry hit some buttons on the lighting box, and the suite came alive with neon. Everything in the main room was pink, black, white or silver. The large, circular, black velvet sofa had pink neon lighting under it giving the appearance of floating on a cloud. The same pink neon came from under the bar top and washed the color down on the small, silver mosaic tiles that covered the front of the bar. The plate glass mirror behind the bar was framed in a simple, wide silver frame and reflected the room making it seem immense. Although the ceiling had appeared to be white initially, now that the drapes kept the daylight at bay, it was reflecting a silver shimmer. Wall sconces washed the silver gray walls, warming it up slightly. Everywhere you looked the chrome and glass reflected the pink neon making the room surreal.

"Henry, we're ready," Candy announced.

"Gentlemen, I shall leave you in their very capable hands. Mr. Colotta will join you for dinner at eight in the VIP dining room located behind the main dining room. The hostess will direct you," said Henry.

I dropped the fluffy white robe and hopped aboard the massage table. Laura began with my shoulders and I could feel the knots releasing with every stroke. For such a tiny lady, she had some powerful hands. The last thing I remember I had flipped over and she was stretching my neck. I woke two hours later still draped on the massage table. The ladies were gone and Roy was snoring peacefully under his blanket. I threw my robe on and poured myself a brandy. All the liquor was top shelf in the bar. I had forgotten how much I loved Vegas. Roy began to stir.

"Hey there buddy, can I offer you something from the bar?

He mumbled something incoherent and rose from the table like Moby Dick breaking the surface of the ocean. "What time is it? How long was I out? Oh my God, I should marry that woman."

"One question at a time, Roy. It's nearly seven so we have an hour before we meet Tony for dinner. Now I'm going to take a healthy shit and start getting dressed for dinner."

"Tony sure knows how to treat special guests," Roy said.

"Keep that in mind Roy. No power; no perks," I said as I disappeared with my brandy into my bedroom. I read 'Playboy' and 'GQ' for the fashion. Nothing looks or feels better than a custom-tailored suit with a custom-made dress shirt in colors and patterns not available from department stores. The acceptable business suit was black or navy blue with a white shirt, fortunately my business afforded me the opportunity to dress to suit myself. Mom used to call me a peacock and she was right. I was a peacock, another tactic I learned from Tony. He was always impeccably dressed with a flair for the dramatic. When he walked into a room, he owned it and it started with his attention-getting wardrobe. Of course I couldn't get away with wearing a pink sports coat, but I did stretch the limits of acceptable dress in my small town. BUT, I was in Vegas now. I didn't need to tone it down here. My jacket was a canary yellow with white pants and a yellow and white print shirt. White shoes were the finishing touch. I looked every bit the Vegas casino owner.

Chapter 6

Vegas

The Flamingo Hotel and Casino

We arrived in the Flamingo's main dining room at ten till eight. The hostess seemed to know instantly who we were. "Mr. Leslie, Mr. Drucker please follow me. Mr. Colotta is expecting you," she said as she led us toward the back of the lounge. She was a delight to follow. Her perfectly round ass cheeks just begged to be grabbed. I made a mental note that I must be feeling the need for some female companionship; a problem easily solved in Vegas.

"Don, Roy, I hope you're finding everything satisfactory. This is my....fixer....Mr. Smith. I thought he might be of some assistance so I asked him to join us." Mr. Smith's custom suit, silk shirt and Italian loafers still couldn't erase the feeling of danger that arose when you looked at him.

The hostess that seated us remained in the room. "Dry martini with two olives for Don, and scotch and soda for Roy. Did I get that right fellas?" he asked.

"Perfect," replied Roy.

She disappeared, but soon there were bustling waiters delivering various appetizers and entrees to the table. After reappearing with drinks, she was dismissed and the four men sat alone in the room.

"Don tells me we have a problem," Tony began.

"That fuckin' Post writer has got the whole town pissed off. It wouldn't have been so bad, but he basically called the people of Terre Haute degenerates who didn't care about crime or were too lazy to do anything about it. Now the citizens are screaming mad and they're backing this little dick running against me in November." Roy complained.

"You've been a good friend to us, and we're not going to let you face this challenge alone. What do you know about this guy at the Post? How did Terre Haute get on his radar? Tony asked.

"I don't know anything about him," Don replied.

"Neither do I," said Roy.

"Well it seems to me the first thing we need is a little research on the author and then let's take a look at the skeletons in Johnson's closet. Mr. Smith, will you start that process. We should get together again after the floor show and discuss this a little further. Do whatever it takes, you understand?" Tony ordered, directing his last comment to Mr. Smith who immediately rose and left the group. When he stood he towered over the table like a gigantic monolith.

"Let's enjoy this meal. I'm afraid I have a meeting afterwards, but you guys can hit the casino floor or whatever you'd like to do. Henry can find you suitable companionship any time; just give him a call. Relax and refresh. This is just a bump in the road. We'll meet here after the 12:00 o'clock floor show."

Tony spent the better part of the next hour plying Roy with booze and reassuring him repeatedly that this wasn't a big problem. Finally Roy was relaxed and ready to gamble.

"If poker is your game, we have a high stakes game you might like. Just show them your room key card, and they'll let you sit in on any game in the house," said Tony. "Food and drinks are on me. Gamble at your own risk, fellas." Tony winked as he stood and buttoned his jacket. "Excuse me, I have to make my rounds now. See you after the show."

I sat quietly and watched as Roy devoured the remaining crab legs and polished off two more scotch and sodas. Roy was too involved with his food to need conversation. It was a wonder to me he didn't explode. Roy opted for some action at the black jack table. I had a different kind of action in mind so I gave Henry a call when I got back to the room.

"Yes Mr. Leslie. What can I do for you? Asked Henry.

"I think a little female companionship is warranted."

"Would that be you and Mr. Drucker?"

"No, just me."

"To serve you better, may I ask you a few questions, sir?

"Certainly."

"What ethnicity would you prefer?"

"White."

"Color of hair?"

"Blonde."

"Build?"

"Slim, but a nice round ass please."

"Any special requirements, sir?"

"No Henry, old fashioned sex is just fine with me."

"I'll have someone sent to your room within the hour, sir."

"Thanks Henry. You're the man!" Now was a good time to try out those magnificent lights Henry demonstrated, so I started playing with combinations till I achieved a perfect level of lighting. In less than an hour there was a knock on the door. I opened the door and there she stood;

perfect in every way. “Hello, hello. Please come in.”

“Don, can I call you Don, Henry sent me.” She purred more than spoke.

“You look fabulous. May I fix you a drink? She was gorgeous. Her blonde hair shimmered when the spotlights over the bar hit it. Her kelly green dress hugged her body like a second skin, accentuating that perfectly round ass. My man Henry strikes again. He is good. She followed me to the bar and slithered onto the barstool. “What is your preference Miss….?”

“Honey. Can you fix a white Russian?” She answered.

“Absolutely, Honey”. I am not one to dish the details but let me say that Honey was very, very nice. It was an evening well spent. Just as Honey was leaving, Roy arrived.

“Thank you darling,” I said as I gave Honey a peck on the cheek. She passed Roy coming down the hall who gave her a well-deserved glance back.

“I see you’ve been busy this evening. So have I. Six thousand dollars busy,” he bragged as he fanned his bankroll at me.

"We've got about an hour before the midnight floor show. Let's clean up and get down before the good seats are taken," I said.

We met in the living room. Roy looked about as good as Roy could look. I was resplendent in a navy jacket with a thin thread of light blue intertwined. I slipped the diamond embellished cigarette case into my breast pocket. I liked diamonds. I particularly liked the way the large diamond ring weighed down my ring finger on my right hand. A man needs well-manicured nails if he intends to wear rings. Roy didn't, and shouldn't, wear rings.

"Let's hit it, Don." He led the way down the brightly colored hallway.

The showroom was ablaze with mirrored balls reflecting the colored lights into the audience. A large pink, lighted flamingo framed the stage. As soon as we entered, the hostess greeted us by name and ushered us to our table, front and center of the stage. We had hardly sat down when the waitress was delivering a martini and scotch and soda.

"Don, I could get used to this," Roy whispered just as the lights dimmed and the master of ceremony entered the stage.

"Ladies and gentlemen, we have a wonderful show for you tonight." Only in Vegas can a man get away with wearing a pink sequined jacket. He carried it off well. "Let's start tonight's show with the famous Flamingo dancers." The dancers lined either side of the flowing staircase to the stage.

Pink and white ostrich plumes jutted from their heads and butts and their pink sequin G-strings and pasties covered the essential parts. They dripped in garish rhinestone necklaces and earrings. Rhinestone bracelets covered their long, pink gloves. The flood lights on the stage reflected the shimmer from the rhinestones and sequins into the audience. They strutted, more than danced, which brought no complaints from the assembled crowd. No one came to see dancers anyway. The neon flamingo frame around the stage, and the reflected grandeur of the ladies, created the stereotypical stage show that sets Las Vegas apart from any other town.

Answering to the loud applause of the crowd, the master of ceremony returned to the stage and announced our star of the show. "It is my pleasure to introduce master magician, Richard Greeno, and his Wonderful World of Magic." I loved magic and had joined a magic club when I was in high school. I had met Richard years before when he came to

Terre Haute and played at the Indiana State Auditorium. He was from Vegas, loved performing magic, and was a party animal; all things I admired so we had shared dinner and a few drinks. I had no idea he would be at the Flamingo performing.

The stage lights went dark, and the center of the stage exploded like a giant sparkler, spewing golden sparks toward the ceiling. In one well-timed movement, the sparkler stopped, and Richard appeared in the spotlight wearing a gold and black brocade tuxedo jacket. The crowd erupted in a warm welcome. His lovely assistant and wife, Nancy, entered from stage left as the stage lights came up. Besides serving as a beautiful prop in the show, she was also the disappearing girl in the box, and the victim of the "saw the girl in half" trick.

His execution was flawless as usual. He did all the usual magic tricks with rings, balls, coins and scarves, but my favorite magic trick was the fish bowl. He always saved the fish bowl for the end. The bowl sat center stage, spotlighted, with a large gold fish swimming nonchalantly in the water. He covered it with a scarf, uttered the magic words and waved his wand. Removing the scarf revealed no fish and no water. In its place was a very confused baby rabbit sitting in the fish bowl. The crowd loved it.

The waitress who had kept our drinks refilled all evening was back at the table. "Gentlemen, Mr. Colotta is waiting. If you'll follow me. I'll see that you have fresh drinks waiting for you at your table." We followed her behind the stage, down a hallway and into a private office. There was a large, round table in the middle of the room seating eight, and a private bar in one corner. The opposite corner contained four easy chairs with a coffee table. There was an entire wall of monitors showing the hallway to the room, the stage, the bar, and all the entrances into the showroom, plus two general audience shots.

Tony sat in one of the easy chairs and Mr. Smith sat in the other. Roy and I took the two remaining chairs. Drinks were already on the coffee table for us.

"Thanks Susan, we'll take it from here. See that we're not disturbed," Tony requested. Susan nodded and left the room. "How's your stay fellas?" Tony asked.

"Tony, It's been amazing," Roy said. "I had good luck at the blackjack table and the company has been super."

"You know Roy, when you are a needed part of the operation, we take good care of you.

Common citizens don't get this kind of treatment." Tony leaned forward and picked up his drink as he paused to let Roy consider what he just said. "You want to keep getting special treatment, don't you Roy?"

"I do. You know I love what I do, but this little prick has got me on the ropes," Roy replied. "He's aggressive as hell. A real go-getter."

"Let's face it Mayor Drucker. You've been mayor for twenty-eight years, and most of that time you've had little competition for the job. I think you just forgot what's involved in a real political race. Maybe there is something we can do to help make this election a little easier for you. Mr. Smith why don't you give us a report on what you found," requested Tony.

"Yes sir. We can't touch the author of the Saturday Evening Post article. Ernest Dobbs is squeaky clean. A real crusader. An ex-war correspondent who has a stellar reputation for finding the truth." Mr. Smith reported. "But, Johnson is another story. Until about three months ago he was Joe Schmoo who worked as a supervisor at the Terre Haute House. The real power behind Johnson is an old acquaintance of yours, Sammy, the Slammer, Cook."

“Shit, I know that name.”

“I’ll bet you do. Your little prick has some very nasty company Mayor. Let me remind you who Sammy is. Sammy and Joey Johnson from Chicago, two guys from Indy, and Irwin and I were arrested in a sting on a bookie operation we were running in Terre Haute. The two guys from Indy had their own attorneys and managed to get off without jail time. Don connected us with a friendly judge in Terre Haute and Irwin and I got off with no jail time. Sammy depended on the mob in Chicago who suddenly forgot who he was. He did eighteen months on a three year sentence. He’s bitter about the way things unfolded.” Tony said.

“I remember Sammy.” I recalled. “He was pretty cocky about his Chicago connections and didn’t need the help of, how did he put it, some small town hustler. Oh yeah, I remember him.”

“Now that we know the power behind little Dick, we need to decide how to work that in our favor,” said Tony. “How do you think the irate citizens of Terre Haute would feel if they knew that little Dick was mobbed up? Tony hit the button of the intercom. “Susan, get Gary in here.”

Mr. Smith had vacated his seat and was behind the bar fixing drinks. It seems he was a man of many talents. When Gary entered, Tony motioned toward the empty seat. "Gary, this is Don and Roy, friends of mine."

"Nice to meet you Don, Roy, extending his hand." He settled into the chair.

"Gary takes care of our special financial arrangements to keep this operation going," Tony explained. That was Vegas speak for handling all the bribes and payoffs necessary so the cops stay off your back. Everyone was so fucking polite to each other. These guys held the power of destroying lives, but the picture they presented to the public was so opposite. I have to admit I admired their dual personalities. They made contributions to charities, and held desert burials for anyone who crossed them.

"What can I do for you, sir?" Gary asked. He didn't waste time on small talk.

"Gary, I need a hundred fifty thousand dollars transferred from one of the mob-friendly banks in Chicago to Pete Johnson in Terre Haute, Indiana. Make sure there is an obvious audit trail back to the Chicago operation. I don't want there to be any doubt about where the money came from," Tony instructed Gary.

"Is that all, sir," Gary asked.

"For right now. Thanks."

Gary got up to leave the room, and Mr. Smith returned to the vacated seat.

"Doesn't he need to know his bank information and stuff," Roy asked.

"Gary is quite capable. "He'll get what he needs," Tony explained. "Now that we have a sizeable contribution from our Chicago friends, we need to find someone to discover this. Mr. Smith, take the jet to Terre Haute in the morning and see what you can find out about little Dick and Sammy. Oh, we'll also need a local reporter. Give me a call when you have some info."

"Got'cha, boss." Mr. Smith rose from the chair and left the room. I noticed how well he filled the doorway of the room as he ducked to make sure he didn't hit the frame. He almost had to turn side ways to get out.

"Tony, I've been giving the Mayor's campaign some thought. Instead of trying to deny the gambling or put a positive spin on it, I think we should ignore it entirely and focus on the good things that have been accomplished under the Mayor," I explained.

"Good plan. The less said in defense of little Dick's accusations, the better. Start making a list of all the things the Mayor has accomplished in his tenure. Roy, you'll have to get your campaign manager to shift gears." Tony advised. "After we spend some time talking about all his accomplishments, the mob connection for little Dick should be leaked. Make sure that you take the high road, at least at first. We don't have proof of anything, yadda, yadda, yadda. Then after more proof starts coming to the surface you can talk about how we have to be careful of supposed reformers with agendas of their own. That sort of thing. I think that coupled with the constant barrage of your good deeds should convert even the most hard-headed native."

"Tony, you're amazing. I'm feeling much better about this whole thing," Roy confessed.

"I've got a lot to do tomorrow. We've got some big players coming in that require a little extra attention. Why don't you fellas just entertain yourselves tomorrow and we'll try to meet up for breakfast before you leave on Sunday. If you need anything, just contact Henry," explained Tony. "It's late now so I need to make my final rounds."

I followed Roy down the hall. The glamourous girls were gone. The flamingo frame looked awkward and boring with no lights, and the crowd of appreciative party goers had been replaced by the cleaning crew and bright lights. We headed up to the room. “You know, I think I’ll check out the swimming pool tomorrow.”

“That sounds good”, said Roy.

Chapter 7

HOME AGAIN, HOME AGAIN

Indiana Theatre, Terre Haute, IN

I got up at noon, took a shower and put on my swim suit. I couldn't help but notice I looked pretty damn good for a guy forty years old. I walked out into the living room carrying my robe and a book.

"Christ Don, is that what you're wearing? Roy asked. He was parked behind the bar and obviously just rolled out of bed. His gray hair stood up on end like a rooster's comb. "Need a little hair of the dog that bit you?"

"No thanks. For your information, this is straight from the Flamingo Men's Shop and I love it. Doesn't leave much to the imagination though, does it?" The gold lame^ speedo only accentuated all my parts; it might have been less revealing to just go commando. "You coming down to the pool?" I asked.

"I think I'm going to hang out here a while. I'm nursing a bit of a hangover. I might hit the black jack tables later if I'm feeling a little better," Roy said.

"Suit yourself. I'll be back in time to clean up for dinner." I headed out the door to the pool with my fluffy robe covering my new suit, feeling quite pleased with myself.

The VIP pool was located on the other side of the flamingo viewing area. The live flamingos strutted around the private fenced island with its own pond in full view of the human inhabitants, but safely separated. I found a chaise in a prime location for viewing, lotioned up, and stretched out on the chaise. As I watched the big pink birds I noted how they didn't fit anyone's concept of a bird. God truly had a sense of humor when he designed these pink feathered birds on stilts. The sun felt great on my skin and I swear I could smell the martinis leaking from my pores. I opened up "The Untouchables" by Eliot Ness and started reading.

I must have nodded off, but woke up when Henry spoke. "Mr. Leslie, is there anything I can get you? Maybe an appetizer and a drink?"

"Henry, you must read minds. I'm getting a bit dry and I could certainly use something to nibble," I said.

"How about some shrimp cocktail or maybe some pickled herring."

"I think a shrimp cocktail and a martini would hold me over nicely until dinner," I said. Henry disappeared to make that happen, and I went back to reading my book. Within five minutes I had a martini and a delightful array of shrimp circling the cocktail sauce, delivered pool side to me. I was enjoying my snack when Roy appeared.

"Thought I'd check on you. Make sure you're not burning to a crisp," he said and sat down on the chaise next to mine.

"Want some?"

"No thanks. I'm going to hit the buffet in a minute. I just came by to see how you were doing," he repeated.

"How were the tables?"

"I'm down about two thousand dollars but I'm still playing on their money so I'm ok."

"I think I'm going to clean up and find a poker game. I'm not as good at laying around as I thought I was. What's your next move?" I asked.

"I think I'll take a little walk outside. Check out what's happening on the strip. Want to meet for dinner at the steakhouse?" about seven?"

"Works for me," I said.

When I got back to the room, I changed clothes and struck out to find a good poker game. I had about twenty thousand dollars with me; not enough for the high rollers of course, but respectable for a normal game. The poker room escaped the Flamingo's pink-washed décor of the other rooms at the hotel, thank God. There were leather barrel chairs surrounding each table and an English library feel to the room. I cruised through the room and picked a likely table. "May I join you?" I asked. The dealer nodded, I handed in five thousand dollars for chips and settled in my seat.

Three hours later, Roy popped into the poker room and tapped his watch to let me know I was running late. I finished up the hand and headed for the cashier. I left with seven thousand eight hundred and ninety dollars.

The casino floor was alive with players; lights flashing and bells ringing. We weaved around the casino floor until we came upon the steakhouse. Our pictures must have been circulated throughout because this hostess greeted us by name too. "Mr. Leslie, Mr. Drucker let me show you to your table," she said. I don't know where Tony finds these women with such lovely round asses, but it makes following these young ladies a treat. I ordered a twenty ounce porterhouse with all the trimmings and, of course, a martini. Roy opted for a filet and scotch and soda. Full of good food and good drink, I was feeling a relaxing evening in the room.

"You know I think I've had about as much of the high life as I can stand," Roy admitted.

"I agree, a quiet evening in the room would suit me. Our plane leaves at 9:30 tomorrow and I want to get breakfast before we leave. That shit they give you on the plane is inedible," I groused.

"I'm not ready for breakfast until about noon, but I could use a few extra z's," said Roy. That was perfect. I could meet Tony as he requested for breakfast, alone.

Tony was already sitting at the table, looking like he just stepped out of a magazine in his white jacket and pink flowered shirt. I appreciated his style. I don't know how he could look so rested when I knew he had been up till all hours working the casino floor?

"Morning Don. Glad you were able to make it without Roy in tow. I wanted a chance to talk to you alone. I know you and Roy have a long history, and we're going to do everything we can to make sure he stays in power. Despite our efforts, there is a good chance that we might not be able to save the good Mayor, and I need to know....If this goes to hell, where do you stand?" he asked. Tony never wasted a lot of time in preliminaries; always right to the point.

"You should know Tony, my loyalties are always going to be with you and the Company. I brought Roy out here to give you a heads up as much as to help get him re-elected. I'm concerned because Roy seems to be losing his edge. I've never seen him so nervous, and he's lost his focus." I explained.

"It might be necessary to remove the Mayor and concentrate on forming a new alliance with Mr. Johnson," he said.

"When you say remove, you're not talking about permanently eliminating him, are you? I won't stand for that Tony. Roy's a good friend to me." I insisted. I hoped my voice didn't show the panic I felt at the thought of permanently eliminating Roy.

"No, no Don. I didn't mean that. I meant excluding him from the inner circle of friends." Tony explained. I suspected that was exactly what he meant, and he was feeling me out to see just how far I was willing to go, if Roy became a problem.

"Roy will willingly retire without revealing anything about the Company. Fortunately, he doesn't know much to reveal. I don't discuss company business with anyone, not even Roy. That's why you have me. The bridge between the Company and the power brokers of Terre Haute. No one knows details about our business." I assured Tony. "I think you can see, Roy still isn't one hundred percent sold on tackling another election. He's gotten pretty comfortable after 28 years."

"Have you ever thought of being mayor of Terre Haute, Don? It wouldn't hurt to have a Company man in that position." Tony asked.

"No. No way. I prefer to manipulate rather than be manipulated. I appreciate everything the Company has done for me, and I would, of course, do whatever they decided was necessary. I really think my talents can best serve the Company where I am." I replied. I had thought of being mayor, but there are entirely too many eyes on the mayor. I lot more can be done out of the public's eye.

"You're right. You're a big help to us where you are. I just wanted to make sure you had no aspirations we were ignoring. I want to keep you happy, too." He assured me. "We'll keep in touch about this situation, of course."

"Tony, your hospitality has been greatly appreciated. It's nice to see you in person on occasion, and I'm sure Roy was impressed." I said.

"Anytime you want to come to Vegas, the suite is yours."

The breakfast was extraordinary and it was good to clear the air with Tony, but it was time to load up for the trip home. I excused myself and again thanked Tony for the wonderful weekend.

Roy was up and dressed. He had fixed coffee so I grabbed a cup. "I see the old bear has finally left his cave. How you feeling this morning?" I asked.

"It's too fucking early," he complained with a total lack of enthusiasm.

"Too much booze and night life makes Roy a grumpy guy," I teased. There was a knock on the door and I was not a bit surprised to find Henry there with two lovely ladies in tow.

"Sir, may I assist you in packing? He asked. This guy does everything but powder your butt! "Why don't you relax while I gather your belongings?" At that, he directed a young lady to each bedroom to begin the packing process.

"Henry is there anything you don't do at this hotel? I hope Tony appreciates what a valuable employee you are." I commented.

"I assure you, sir, I am well compensated for my efforts. It doesn't hurt if you would let him know I adequately addressed your needs." He advised.

"Henry I think you should join us for some coffee while the girls finish their duties. Have a seat and let me get you a coffee. Cream or sugar?" I asked as I patted the bar stool.

"Sir, I really shouldn't." Henry sat with a little more encouragement. "I don't normally fraternize with the guests." He explained.

"Just think of us as two guys who have forced you to participate in a going away ritual. We absolve you of all guilt." I promised, sitting the coffee in front of him.

"Come on, Henry, I know there's a real person in there somewhere. He wants out," added Roy.

Henry relaxed a bit; only a bit. We talked for a little while, but had to cut it short when the girls appeared at the bedroom doors with suitcases on trolleys, ready to depart. Just as I was getting to know ol' Henry too.

"Ah, sirs, we're ready to go. Please check your suites and make sure we have gotten all your belongings." He advised.

As directed, we reviewed the bedroom suites. There was nothing left behind. We started down the hall; Henry, then Roy and I, and then the two ladies with their trollies, looking like a full entourage of very important people. When we exited the elevator there was a limo waiting at the curb.

"Henry, it has been my absolute pleasure to meet you. I hope to see you again on my next trip to Vegas," I said as I climbed into the limo.

"I have enjoyed meeting you as well, Mr. Leslie," Henry turned to shake Roy's hand. "And you Mr. Drucker."

The first class trip home was uneventful with the exception of Roy's bitching about the food provided. He managed to choke it down with two scotch and sodas. I laid off and just had coffee. Most of the way home I ruminated about my discussion with Tony. There is always more underlying information than what is actually said during these conversations. Roy, clueless about our trip, was just feeling happy and relaxed. Good for him.

Chapter 8

The Girls are Coming

Dad's Cadillac, the "Banana Boat"

I was having the time of my life. I knew people from everywhere. My bonding business was flourishing. I had every case in Terre Haute from wife beaters to murderers, most of whom never skipped out. Occasionally, I'd have to track down Old Joe, a frequent flyer who lost his license years ago, but continued to drive....badly. The housewives and old ladies that lost their allowances at the keno game loved me, and I took care to charm them all. The politicians on the tab to keep the doors open, respected the additional tax-free bonus money I provided. It was a win/win for everyone, and I was enjoying life to the fullest. Having money and reputation is an easy in with the dames too. I had women fawning all over me.

Mom lived with me after Dad died and took care of all the necessary household duties. She cooked, cleaned and did my laundry and I provided a gorgeous new brick home with an in-ground swimming pool and extended visits with her two granddaughters. My girls, came over every summer and spent a couple of months with us.

We didn't move anything old into the new house. The old furniture we had for more than ten years and came from Mom and Dad's house. There was a very scratchy beige mohair sofa and chair with enormously wide arms, and a hodge-podge of end tables. There was no formal dining room furniture; only a red and white chrome kitchen set with a gray Formica top. Mom's bedroom was made of blonde Formica and consisted of a triple dresser, upright chest and a bed with a bookcase headboard. My bedroom furniture was the same furniture I had from the time I was a teenager; indestructible maple with oversized knobs. It had to go: All of it.

When you entered the new house you were greeted with a small foyer. The main part of the house was wide open. The kitchen overlooked the dining room which was adjacent to the living room. A huge picture window in the living room coupled with the sliders leading from the dining room to the pool, created a wonderful light-filled living space. I furnished the living room with the latest ultra-modern platform sofas. The platforms extended on either side creating the end tables on which resided tall, walnut lamps. I guess you would call it mid-century modern but I just called it sexy.

We had a proper dining table with six chairs and there was a bar that separated the kitchen from the dining room where there were four stools. All the appliances were top-of-the-line. My bedroom was purple and black. Mom made me a purple bedspread with a large, black "D" in the center. All my bedroom furniture was black lacquer. Mom's room was pretty and pastel, as you might expect, and had a pink flowered comforter and curtains. The girls shared bunk beds in the third bedroom since it was the smallest room and they were only there occasionally on weekends and a couple months each summer.

My girls, now fourteen and sixteen, came over to spend two months with me in the summer of 1963, and it gave me a great opportunity to wow them.

"I'm going to take you and the girls out for dinner tonight and show them around Terre Haute a little" I told Mom. "Why don't you take them shopping and get their hair done today. Be ready about 6 tonight."

"I'll call Saucy Curls and get an appointment and then we'll go to Meis and get a pretty summer dress for each of them," Mom added.

"Thanks Mom. Here's four hundred dollars. Get yourself something pretty too." I got up and gave her a kiss.

Neither of my girls had ever been to a hair salon before. Their mom always cut their hair. The current fad, I was told, was a "poodle do". The look consisted of a semi-short haircut tightly curled all over with a perm, making it look very similar to a poodle's butt…..who am I to judge fashion?

When I picked up the girls they looked darling. "Wow, who are these good looking women?

"Dad we had the best time today. Grandma took us to a salon and then shopping. We met the elevator lady as Meis. You should see the elevator. It looks like a big, brass birdcage and she has this big round thing she uses to stop on the floors you want. It's awesome," Donna said. The kids kept chattering about their day as we walked to the car.

"We have to pick up a friend of mine for dinner so we best hurry," I urged.

I introduced the girls to Eleanor. She was beautiful in a mature way. The big rock on her hand, and the mink stole draped across her shoulders made her look even more like a gangster's moll. She would ultimately be wife number five. I found her to be a good match. She could drink like a man, swear like a trucker, clean up nicely and because she was the hostess at the Saratoga Restaurant we knew a lot of the same people.

I took everyone across the state line to a little place in Paris, IL that had the best lobster. It was a plain ugly building outside and required entry through a doorman. Inside was different.

"Look at the lobsters. They're enormous," Pat said. She was so fascinated by the size and the fact they were alive in a large tank, it was hard to get her to her seat.

"Hello again, Mr. Leslie. So good to see you," greeted the Host. "Let me show you to your table."

The Host settled the girls into their chairs and they giggled and exchanged looks.

“Pete, we’re celebrating tonight. Bring us two martinis and champagne for the girls, please,” I requested. I knew that would impress them.

Dinner in Paris, Illinois, our first stop of the night.
(left to right) Mom, Donna, Pat, Eleanor and me

“Are we allowed?” whispered Donna.

“Only when you’re with me” I said.

The girls had surf and turf and had a bite of my pickled herring, although that was greeted with disgust. They thoroughly enjoyed the champagne though.

After a leisurely dinner, we loaded back into the big yellow Cadillac convertible. “Please can we put the top down?” they cried in unison.

“After we drop off Mom and Eleanor, we can,” I replied.

I walked Eleanor to the door, gave her a lingering kiss and walked back to the car sensing my girls had been properly impressed. Mom was tired. It had been a big day for her, and it was time for her to turn in for the night.

“OK kiddos, it’s time to show you a little bit of Terre Haute,” I said. I dropped the top on the convertible and Pat squealed. “We have to make a stop along the way.”

The Caddie arrived in front of a small green house with a big front porch, and Sally came running from the house and jumped into the front seat. She was younger than Eleanor and prettier. She hadn’t been beaten down by an ex-husband and three kids so she was far happier too. She had long, dark hair that seemed to welcome the airy convertible.

"Hi kids, your Dad's told me so much about you. I'm Sally."

"I'm showing the kids the nightlife in Terre Haute so I thought we'd go to the Idaho Club." I said. Sally was always ready for a good time.

"Great!"

The Idaho Club

The Idaho Club was a nightclub at 719 Hulman Street with pink and blue neon banding around the otherwise nondescript front of the building. We pulled around to the darkened parking lot in the back of the building.

Opening the back door, we were greeted by Boomer, a hunk of a man who handled any disturbance quickly and quietly. "Hey Don. Who are the beautiful ladies with you?"

"These are my daughters, Boomer. Donna and Pat. We're celebrating tonight so find us a special seat will you?"

"You bet. Nothing but the best for such lovely ladies," he said directing us to a corner booth with a perfect view of the stage, but in a darkened area in the back. A great location for looking, but not necessarily being seen.

"Don, nice to see you again," greeted Denise. "What can I get you all to drink?"

"Denise, I'll have a martini and a grasshopper for Sally. How about a couple of Shirley Temples for the girls, maybe slip a splash of rum in to warm them up a little," I winked at Denise.

"Sure thing Don. Coming right up."

"Wait till you girls see the stage show here." It was a little risqué for teenagers, but I was sure the girls could handle it.

As the lights on the stage came up, they bounced off the silver bikinis on the girls. They proceeded to strut around the stage and sing the opening song. I looked at the girls who were both staring wide-eyed at the silver-accented display of womanly flesh. They completed their song and introduced the star of the show, a Frank Sinatra look-a-like who also sounded like ole Blue Eyes.

The girls sipped their drinks while Sally and I had another, and listened to the star finish up his set with 'My Way'. "They'll play this at my funeral," I added. When he was finished he came over to the table.

"Don, how nice to see you. Who are these beautiful young ladies?" he asked.

"My daughters, Donna and Pat." I motioned to each of the girls.

My daughter Donna was nearly drooling at the handsome star with his curly black hair and steel blue eyes. This did not go unnoticed by "Frank".

"Would you mind if your daughter helps me out in the next set?" He asked and I thought Donna was going to faint.

"Actually we're celebrating tonight and I can't think of a better way to do that. Sure she'll help," I said.

Before she had time to object, he scooped her up off the booth and drug her onto the stage. "Guys, can we get a barstool for this lovely lady? Ladies and gentlemen, Donna has consented to help me out with this next song," Frankie announced

Frankie began a rendition of "Fly me to the Moon" sung directly to Donna as her face turned beet red and she gazed adoringly into his eyes. When he walked behind the stool and wrapped his arms around her, I thought she was going to faint. This would be a night she won't forget. Score one for Dad!

Frankie returned Donna to the booth after the song, kissed her hand and thanked her for her assistance. Donna drank the remainder of her Shirley Temple in one gulp. "Wow, my daughter is a star!"

"Oh my God, Dad. He's so dreamy. I could just die," she said.

There was more floor show, but I'm pretty sure from the look on Donna's face, she didn't see any of it. It was nearly 2 now and it was approaching last call, not that it mattered to us, but it was time to wrap it up for the night.

"Thanks for a lovely evening, Don. You girls, it was great meeting you. Maybe I'll see you again, Sally said as she jumped from the car and fairly skipped to the front porch of her house, waving as she reached the door.

"Have you girls had a good time, tonight? I asked.

"Oh gosh, yes," they exclaimed in unison.

"Let me make a quick phone call here." We pulled over into a closed gas station and I stepped out to make a call. After verifying my friend was home and willing for a little late night company, we had our third stop of the night.

"One more stop, kids," I implored.

This time we all got out of the car and went up the stairs to the second floor apartment. I knocked on the door and Tammy opened the door dressed in a very respectable night gown covering all the necessities.

"Hi, sweetheart," I said as we all piled into the apartment. These are my daughters, Donna and Pat. Kids this is Tammy, a friend of your Daddy's."

Tammy had milk and cookies set up in the kitchen for the kids, and I parked them there and disappeared in the bedroom with Tammy, reappearing in about half an hour, feeling refreshed and relaxed. Pat had fallen asleep on the sofa in the living room, but Donna was still in the kitchen. She gave me a knowing wink which made me slightly uncomfortable. I guess at sixteen she knows what happens when the kids get milk and cookies.

"Thanks, honey," I said and gave her a kiss goodbye and a friendly pat on her butt. "Let's go kids. Thank Tammy for the milk and cookies."

"Thanks, Tammy," they said in chorus.

"Hey Dad can we sit on the back of the car like they do in the parades," Pat asked.

"Sure. Just don't fall."

The girls sat on the boot of the convertible and waved at the imaginary crowd. Everyone seemed pretty tired when we got home. It was after 4 a.m. by this time. Time for all of us to hit the hay.

The next morning I woke to the excited voices of my kids, telling Mom about the naked, silvery women. Breakfast was totally ignored as the girls shared their big night out in Terre Haute. I was met with a disapproving look from Mom, but she said nothing....literally nothing.

Chapter 9

My Greatest Regret

We had a big crowd at the Keno game the night it happened, and three of my checkers were down with the flu. I had to pull two of my workers from the kitchen to be checkers, leaving Ron by himself to run the kitchen. By the end of the evening, we were all bone tired so I invited the whole staff to breakfast. A few opted to go home, but a group of ten joined me for breakfast at the Waffle House. We spent a couple of hours hashing over the evening, and congratulating each other on a job well done. I left feeling tired and contented. That changed quickly.

As I drove in the driveway I saw a distinct blue smoke coming from under the garage door. I ran into the garage and saw the problem immediately. Mom had left her car running and the garage was full of the blue smoke. I opened the door to turn off the car and that's when I saw her. Mom lay in the backseat of the car. I could tell immediately she was already dead. I checked for a pulse and then went in the house to call Sherriff Wesley.

"John, its Don Leslie. I came home and found my mom dead. I guess I'm going to need the police and coroner," I said trying to sound much steadier than I felt.

"Right away, Don."

I hung up and immediately started sobbing. The police were there within ten minutes and the ambulance very soon after. I wiped my face and hurriedly pulled myself together. The quiet neighborhood was ablaze with red and blue flashing lights. Sheriff Wesley arrived soon after and escorted me into the house.

"I'll handle Mr. Leslie's statement, detectives. You just clear the scene," Wesley ordered.

The coroner arrived shortly after the Sheriff to pronounce Mom dead.

Sheriff Wesley had questions; not nearly as many as I did. Mom often threatened suicide when something happened she couldn't handle. When I decided to marry Eleanor, she was "going to end it all". They were vacant words and we both knew she wouldn't. At least, I thought she wouldn't.

"Don, did your Mom have any concerns?" asked Wesley.

"No, there hasn't been any problems. You know if Mom really hated something she would sometimes say she was going to end it all, but she hadn't mentioned anything like that for at least two years. I don't know what happened to bring this on." I said. My head was pounding and I felt like my world had ended. I just wanted to be alone.

"Where were you, Don?" asked the Sheriff.

"I had a game tonight and then we stopped for breakfast," I explained.

"Do you always stop for breakfast," asked the Sheriff.

"No, actually. We never stop. It was a fluke. We had a tough night and we just needed to unwind a little before we went home," I replied. *A sudden wave of guilt washed over me as the words left my mouth. If only I had come home right after the game. . . .*

"Do you have a funeral home selected? I can call them to pick up your Mother," Wesley inquired.

"Callahan Funeral Home," I replied.

"Don, I'm so sorry about your Mom. We'll get these guys out of here so you can have some private time." He left to coordinate the release of the body and deal with Callahan.

I sat there feeling numb. The tears started flowing and I found myself still sitting in the chair an hour later exhausted from crying. If I just hadn't stopped! What could have happened to push her to try to kill herself? I vowed I'd find out.

****

Eleanor, now officially wife number five, and I arrived with the girls about an hour before the showing. I took the girls up to the casket and explained to them what had happened. Mom looked beautiful. Her white hair was freshly curled and she was wearing the lavender crepe dress she wore to my last wedding. She looked like should could step out of the casket and join us for dinner. I remembered her body in the back seat of the car, already turning black from the carbon monoxide. I was so grateful they were able to restore her for the funeral.

Pat asked, “Why is everyone crying.”

“They’re sad that your Grandma won’t be around anymore and that makes some people cry.” I explained.

“Aren’t you sad? Donna asked.

“I’m very sad. I loved your Grandma very much and I miss her terribly, but men don’t cry in public like women do. We cry privately; when we’re by ourselves.” After the girls said goodbye to their grandma, Eleanor took them to meet their Mother.

I took a final look around the room. There was such an abundance of flowers, almost to the point of embarrassment. Pink roses and star gaze lilies, her favorites, appeared in every manner of arrangement. The largest and most innovative was from Tony. It must have set him back $300. Heather's Flowers can come up with combinations that are totally unique, and she outdid herself. The only arrangement more resplendent was the casket spray also done by her. I had told Heather I wanted star gaze lilies and cabbage roses which she used as the center of the arrangement while tiny lavender and pink roses formed tendrils that fell from the arrangement like a gorgeous waterfall. Nestled in the arrangement was a white satin ribbon with "Mother" on it. It was stunning. Mom would have appreciated her exit appearance.

The four hour visitation was excruciating. Mom knew so many people because of her dress shop and her association with the Eastern Star. All of my associates showed up as did all of the blue hairs from the Keno game. The crowd looked like a who's who in Terre Haute government. I only remember the line never seemed to end. The day was mostly a blur. Everyone did their best to say just the right thing, but I just nodded. It was extremely difficult for me to maintain. At one point Bill Gooding, the funeral director, escorted me to his office just to give me a break. I took advantage of the solitude and broke down for fifteen minutes or so, and then returned to the receiving line.

The Order of the Eastern Star has a moving ceremony performed as part of the funeral. I can't remember all of the wording. There is a lengthy prayer and then each lady places a pink rose in the casket as they leave. Mother wasn't religious and neither of us went to church, but the funeral home arranged for someone to officiate and he did a great job considering he had never met my Mother before.

I went home to an empty house, sat in the dark, and had a good stiff drink; several in fact. The quiet was unbearable. Everywhere I looked, I saw Mom cooking or playing solitaire at the dining table. She played one continuous game of solitaire her entire life. In Vegas style you purchase the deck for $52 and you earned $5 for every card played on the aces. I walked over to the table and there was her tally. She was in debt $13,895. I stood there and looked at the tally sheet. She had the most beautiful handwriting.

The next week I tried to retrace Mom's steps. She didn't keep a written schedule so this wasn't going to be easy. I knew she had her hair done and I could tell from the frig that she had gone to the grocery. I started with Saucy Curls.

I was there at 9:00 a.m. when they opened. “My name is Don Leslie and my mother came here to get her hair done. Could I speak to the manager, please?”

“If you’ll wait here,” asked the receptionist.

“Mr. Leslie, my name is Laura. I own this salon. How can I help you?” she said.

“My Mother has been coming here for several years, Bea Leslie?” I said.

“Yes, of course, Mrs. Leslie is a valuable customer.” commented Laura.

“Is there somewhere more private where we could go?” I asked.

“Certainly, why don’t you come to my office,” replied Laura. I followed her around the corner and into a very feminine office. “Please have a seat Mr. Leslie.”

“The cause of Mom’s death was not common knowledge. Most people just assumed she died of natural causes because of her age, but Mom actually committed suicide. I’m trying desperately to understand her mental status. Something had to happen to bring this on, so I’m retracing her steps to see what might have happened,” I explained.

“The person who would have known her best was her stylist, Peggy. She always saw Peggy for her services. I’ll send her in to talk with you,” she said.

“Mr. Leslie, I’m Peggy Mrs. Leslie’s stylist. How can I help you?” asked Peggy. I remember Mom talking about what wild fashions her stylist wore. Mom undersold Peggy’s appearance. She was no more than 5’ tall but was wearing red platform boots stretching to her mid-thigh making her appear taller. Her short flouncy skirt brushed the top of her boots and was topped with a front-laced, black leather corset. Her hair had that organized ‘I just got out of bed’ look. It was jet black with red streaks. I can see why Mom would have liked her.

“My Mother died last week and I have been trying to retrace her steps to decide what might have upset her to the point she thought she had no alternative but to take her own life. Did Mom express any concerns when she was here?” I asked.

“Oh, Mr. Leslie, I am so sorry. I didn’t know. She was such a cool lady,” she said. “We were always gossiping about the latest escapades of the movie stars. Bea loved those movie magazines, and we had fun making up details behind the headlines that didn't get reported.

"Did anything unusual happen? Did Mom express any concerns or seem unhappy?" I asked

"It was a pretty normal appointment. She was talking about the latest visit from the girls. Just the usual girl talk. Nothing worrisome. She seemed in a great mood."

"Do you know where she was going after her appointment?" I asked.

"Well, she mentioned going to the grocery before she went home. Nowhere else that I remember." Peggy said.

"Peggy, thank you for your time." I appreciate it."

Peggy threw her arms around me as I stood up. "I'm so sorry about Miss Bea. She was such a nice person. I loved seeing her every week," said Peggy, her eyes watering.

I left Saucy Curls and headed toward Kroger in the Meadows Shopping Center. That's where Mom always went for groceries. When I arrived I went straight to the cashier and asked for the manager.

"Mr. Leslie, I'm Harry Satin the general manager. What can I do for you?" Asked Harry.

"My Mother, Bea Leslie, shops here and she was here last week. She came home from shopping and was very upset. I was wondering if there might have been anything unusual happen while she was here," I asked.

"I'm not sure what you mean by unusual," said manager Harry.

"Did she have a confrontation with anyone at the store? Maybe someone else had a fight that upset her?" I asked.

"Not that I am aware of, no."

"Well, thanks anyway for your help." I replied.

"Can I ask why you want to know?" asked Harry.

"Mom died last week and I'm trying to understand what might have contributed to her stress." I replied.

"Sorry I couldn't be of more help, and I'm sorry to hear about your Mother," Harry said. Harry headed back to his office, and I started to leave when one of the cashier's grabbed me by the elbow.

“I know what happened with your Mom,” said the young clerk. “Meet me outside away from the door.”

I lurked far enough away from the front of Kroger to not be seen. The young cashier came out and found me with no problem. She wasted no time. “Mr. Leslie your Mom was arrested last week for shoplifting. Harry took her into the office and they actually called the police. She had put a tube of lipstick into her purse. I don’t think she meant to take it, but Harry wouldn’t listen to her at all. She was bawling when the police came. He didn’t have her arrested on the spot, but told her it would be in the paper and all her friends would know. He was really mean to her and I felt sorry for her,” said the young clerk.

“I want to thank you for telling me.”

“I’ve got to get back to work. I’m sorry about your Mom. She was a really sweet lady,” said the clerk.

I sat in the car and the tears came again. Mom must have been mortified at the thought of her friends seeing her name associated with shoplifting charges. Now I knew what initial blow brought Mom to such desperation. If only I had gone straight home that night. The house was so empty without her.

Chapter 10

Setting the Stage

Auditorium of Indiana State University, Terre Haute, IN

A couple of weeks later I got a call from Tony. “Don, I’m sending Gary and Mr. Smith to Terre Haute this weekend. Do you think you could make some time for them?”

“Sure. Are they staying at The Pick?” I asked.

“Yes. They’ll be in late Friday night. I thought maybe you could meet them for breakfast in the private dining room at ten o’clock. Would that work for you? Tony inquired. “I’ll let them catch you up on all the details. How’s Roy holding up?”

“I’m keeping him busy working with his team to come up with all the good things he’s accomplished over the last twenty-eight years. They’re all excited to have a campaign plan. I’ve done some marketing stuff for them, and it’s at the printers now. I think you’ll be pleased.” I said.

“Great. I’ll tell the boys you’ll be there. Have a productive weekend,” he said as he signed off. Tony was a man of few words, but when he spoke you wanted to make sure to get the whole message.

Saturday morning I headed for The Pick for breakfast in the private dining room. The boys were having coffee when I arrived. After surveying the menu, we all ordered breakfast and made small talk about their flight and accommodations until breakfast was served. "We won't be needing anything else," Gary informed the waitress. "Please see that we aren't interrupted. Thanks."

"Mr. Smith, why don't you bring us up to date with what you've found," Gary said.

"Sure. This Pete Johnson is a simple fellow that Sammy made feel real special when he picked him as the opposing candidate for mayor. He has no background, but he does have a down-home kind of thing going that makes him relatable to the regular folks. Sammy has convinced him he is the savior of Terre Haute and the poor dope believes it. All the "contributions" for the campaign have come directly from Sammy's pockets, with the notable exception of one hundred and fifty thousand dollars from a concerned citizen. His campaign manager is a junior law partner from one of the law firms representing the Chicago mob in real estate deals, and his "staff" consists of some Indiana State students who are using the election as a school project."

"So, we have a guy with no experience, backed by Chicago mobsters, with a campaign manager who works at a mobbed up law firm, and a gang of college students handling his public relations. I'm not seeing a huge threat here," I joked.

"Don't kid yourself, Don. For whatever reason, Chicago has suddenly become interested in Terre Haute, and that is something we really don't want to happen. We want to make sure this remains a Vegas town. Let's hear Smith's report," explained Gary.

"OK, so this guy who wrote the article for the Saturday Evening Post is squeaky clean, but it appears the actual editor of the Post might have an axe to grind with Mayor Drucker. Lewis was a reporter at the Tribune back when Drucker was first elected twenty eight years ago. Seems Drucker fielded a particularly juicy bit of news to another cub reporter, rather than Lewis. The story was picked up nationally and lead to a promotion for said reporter, leaving Lewis out in the cold," Mr. Smith said. "Evidently, Lewis holds a grudge for a long time. When he heard there might be something interesting going on in Terre Haute, he jumped at the chance to smear Drucker, and contacted Ernest Dobbs. He's known for digging to the bottom of the barrel to get all there is to a story. He's your squeaky clean author of the "Sin City" article."

"How is Roy holding up?" Asked Gary.

"He's pretty busy coming up with his master list of things he's accomplished in twenty eight years as mayor." I replied.

"I think it's time to leak our mob connection to the paper. Have you figured out how that's going to work, Smith?" Gary asked.

"Yeah, there's a hot little filly on staff at the television station eager to make a name for herself. As long as we have the proof, she's willing to run with it. There is a packet ready to be delivered to her, giving her all the ammunition she needs to trace the donation and ties to Sammy and Chicago. We just have to drop it in the mail to her. Just say when." Smith said.

"Don, have you seen the latest commercials for Drucker's good deeds? Gary asked.

"No, but I picked up a copy of the proposed announcement after I got Tony's call. We can take a look at it now," I said. I got up and inserted the VCR into the system.

"Your home-town mayor, Roy Drucker, has been in office for the last twenty-eight years. He has attracted seven new factories, and unemployment is at an all-time low. Under Mayor

Drucker's incentives, Indiana State has expanded from a liberal arts teacher's college to a University with a Nursing School, Business College, and pre-law and pre-med degrees. The building of the new School of Business, the Library and the Student Center/Auditorium has changed the look of the area around the school. Downtown businesses have rebuilt after the fire with grants from the city, making downtown a destination again. Let's keep Terre Haute growing. Re-elect Mayor Roy Drucker." As the voice over touted his accomplishments, pictures of Roy at the opening of the Clabber Girl addition, his speech at the College, and the reopening of the downtown shopping district rolled across the screen.

"Well, it's not exactly the most exciting spot I've seen but it's adequate for our purposes." Gary said. "I think it's probably time to move on to step two. Mr. Smith, I think it's time to mail that package to your television reporter. Don, we're going to need you to keep careful tabs on Roy. We can't have him getting panicky and doing something stupid."

"He's run unopposed in the last twelve years, so he's not used to actually campaigning. I'll keep an eye on him, and we've arranged to have dinner once a week to update each other." I said. I was secretly worried that Roy was not putting himself out there like he should. I needed a hundred percent from Roy, and he was giving me about half that. "You know I'll do all I can to keep him in line, Gary."

"Tony trusts you to do what is necessary." "How are the games going?" he asked.

"We have a full house every week. It's been a little tricky keeping everyone happy and off my back, but I'm getting it done." I said. "Things should start easing up once word gets out about the Chicago connection to the little prick."

"I'll hand deliver the envelope to Amanda at WTHR right now," Mr. Smith stated. "I'm pretty sure she'll have it checked out and on the air by Monday. She's pretty sharp. The mountain that was Mr. Smith rose to take care of business as he spoke."

"Why don't I pick you guys up this evening for dinner, say around 7? I said.

"Sure Don, we'll be ready."

Chapter 11

Let's Sling Some Dirt

The Chicago connection story broke on the news that evening, "with more updates to follow" as they say. The initial report caused a multitude of phone calls throughout the political hierarchy. Committee Chairman Lloyd Master immediately called Pete Johnson who of course didn't have a clue, as usual. Sammy got wind and called a meeting with Pete Johnson. I wasn't invited but I think the meeting would have been something like this:

A panic-struck Pete jumps Sammy as soon as he comes into sight. "I got a call from Amanda at channel WTHR this afternoon who wanted me to confirm a contribution I received from some mob-connected group in Chicago. I told her I didn't know anything about any mobsters anywhere."

"She's just trying to rattle you. There is no contribution from Chicago." Sammy assured Pete.

"She says there's one hundred and fifty thousand dollars in an account in my name. What's going on, Sammy? She made out like I'm involved with some really bad people," Pete exclaimed.

"I've got a call in to some people I know to try and find out where she got her information. I need you to stay cool and just refer any questions to me, your new campaign manager. This is nothing but a smear campaign because we're gaining ground over the mayor. If you can't handle the situation, take the wife and kids for a long weekend trip somewhere. I'll handle it and by the time you get back, everything will be quiet again." Sammy assured Pete.

"We'll go visit her mother in Evansville. Call me and let me know what happens."

I'm pretty sure Sammy was immediately on the phone to Chicago to verify who sent the money, but that's a big operation in Chicago and Sammy was not highly regarded. It could take several days before Sammy might connect with anyone who would admit to knowing anything about the money.

The next morning, Amanda continued with a special report directly following the morning news. "Good morning. This morning we have an update on the story we brought you last night. So far we have been unable to identify the anonymous concerned citizen from Chicago who made the $150,000 donation to Pete Johnson's campaign fund; that's a lot of "concern" folks and we have to wonder if some consideration isn't expected for such a generous donation. We can confirm the money came from a bank in Chicago known to be friendly to syndicated crime." Amanda said. "I contacted Mr. Johnson last evening to get his explanation for this contribution. He denied knowing anyone in Chicago, and had no idea he had received any such contribution. Conveniently, he and his family departed for a long weekend in the country last night."

"I also contacted Mayor Drucker to see what he thought of this contribution. The Mayor stated, and I quote, 'I'm sure there is some explanation for this. I can't imagine that Mr. Johnson would take a bribe or contribution from a known criminal. His entire platform hangs on ridding our city of the bums and mobsters who give our city a bad reputation; that's his description not mine."

Amanda carefully followed the audit trail designed for her to find. "Ladies and gentlemen, I have spent the better part of the last two days verifying the information on the mysterious concerned citizen responsible for the one hundred and fifty thousand dollar donation to Pete Johnson's campaign. I can now tell you I have traced it back to a gang in Chicago run by the notorious mobster, Sam Giacana. I have tried repeatedly to contact Mr. Johnson for comment, but he has refused to take my phone calls. He referred me to Sammy Cook, his new campaign manager. I was told by Mr. Cook, and I quote "the contribution we received was anonymous, and there were no strings attached to that donation. You're trying to smear my candidate, and I demand you stop immediately."

Roy and I were having dinner at the Pick, and watching the evening news. Amanda was proving to be invaluable. "Roy, I think it's time for you to issue your second comment on the unfolding scandal surrounding Mr. Johnson." I said. "Let me hear what you have in mind for your next retort."

"Well my line will be that we should be extremely careful of people who present themselves as do-gooders. There are a lot of people willing to prey on the fear of others. They can use that to their advantage, and may have a hidden agenda," Roy said.

"You've got the routine down well. Stay unemotional, but keep repeating that refrain. Then immediately talk about all the good things you've done for Terre Haute," I said.

Roy finished his Swiss steak and got up to leave. I was close behind when Nancy said I had a phone call. I grabbed the house phone and an unfamiliar voice spoke. "Mr. Leslie, I'm a friend of Sam Giacana and we need to talk."

I waved Roy to go ahead and leave. "What can I do for you, friend?"

"Mr. Giacana has become aware that there has been some kind of arrangement with Tony Collota in Vegas which circumvents the usual channels of the Company. We need to rectify that problem. Do you understand? He asked.

"I'm afraid I don't. My contact in Vegas has been working out very well. I'm not sure what arrangements you have with them, but it doesn't involve me. That's entirely up to you guys." I replied.

"I assure you, Mr. Leslie, we have contacted our Vegas branch. This is simply a notification to you that there will be changes coming. We'll talk again soon." He said.

I had a very disquieting feeling after talking to him. Obviously, we had really opened a can of worms. I wasn't sure how Tony planned to deal with this.

Head of the Chicago Organization, Sam Giacana (center)

Chicago's interest in the mayoral election was becoming annoying. As expected, Tony called me.

"Don, Tony here. How you doin'? He said.

"Well things here are getting more intense every day. It seems we awakened Chicago's interest in our activities, and I've been contacted by one of Giacana's men regarding payment arrangements after Johnson takes the election. I told them maybe we should wait until after the election to talk. They're pretty damn sure of themselves." I said. "Way too sure."

"I was afraid that might happen. I inadvertently clued them in to a money trail they didn't know existed. We didn't declare our revenue from Terre Haute, so Chicago didn't get their kickback. Now they're wise, and just like in Vegas, they're claiming a percentage of everything we get. This is not a good situation, Don. It's going to cost both of us money." Tony explained. "It's really irrelevant who wins now, but I can tell you, I don't think they're going to be as easy to work with as me."

"I was very noncommittal when I talked with them." I said.

“It doesn’t matter what you said, Chicago has us in their crosshairs so we’ll pay, period.”

“I don’t know how else we could have handled this, Tony. If we had done nothing, Roy would have lost and we’d be closed down completely. At least this way we have an opportunity to make some money.” I said.

“Yeah, I suppose. It just bugs me that they get a cut of everything even though they contributed no up-front money, and did nothing to develop this relationship. How is Roy holding up? Tony asked.

“He’s ok. We watched the news cast on TV during dinner last night. He’s a little shaky, but he’ll be ok.” I replied. I was less convinced than I sounded.

****

Roy arrived home a little later than normal, and Sarah could tell immediately he was in a mood. “Sarah, bring me a scotch and soda, will you?” Roy said as he sank into his favorite easy chair. It had been another tough day at his office. He was bombarded with calls from Amanda at WTHR as well as some ‘Times’ reporter who wanted comments. He was tired of walking the line between Mr. Mayor, compassionate for his opponent and Mr. Mayor, the aggressive candidate up for reelection. Maybe he was getting too old for this.

"Sarah, no dinner tonight. I've got some paperwork to finish. I'll be in the library. Don't disturb me." Roy demanded. Truthfully he just didn't want to hear her twenty questions about his day. He wasn't up to putting a spin on one more question today.

Sarah stood at the door in disbelief. "I made your favorite; pot roast." She whined.

"I told you, I've got work to do." Rising from his easy chair and bolting for the library door before she could make him feel guilty, he growled "No phone calls; I don't care who." .

He sat behind the old oak partner's desk in his well-worn burgundy leather desk chair. He didn't have any work to do, he just couldn't bear one more question about how his day was going, not even from his lovely wife.

Two hours later, Sarah tapped on the door. "Can I get you some coffee, dear." She asked.

"NO I don't need coffee," he shouted too loud. He already had a scotch and soda, several as a matter of fact. What he needed was a little privacy to unwind.

"I'm going to bed. See you in the morning" Sarah murmured.

Roy sat in his library sipping his drink and rethinking the day. He was tired. Tired of playing cat and mouse with Amanda, tired of humoring me, and tired of his every move being watched and criticized. I knew Roy was not up for this fight, and things had only gotten worse since the scandal broke.

It was 3:00 in the morning when I got the call from Sheriff Wesley. "Don, I'm at Roy Drucker's house. You need to come over here", he said. I wasted no time getting over to Roy's. When I arrived the blue and red lights lined the circular driveway giving it a garish look. There were squad cars, a CSI unit and the coroner's wagon. My heart sank. Sheriff Wesley met me in the driveway.

"I'm sorry, Don. It's a pretty ugly scene in there; best prepare yourself. You need to slip into one of these suits." John said.

John was right. Roy was in his library sitting behind his desk. There was blood and brain matter splattered all over the leaded glass windows behind him. Most of the back of Roy's head was missing, but his scotch and soda still sat on the desk intact. His right hand hung at his side and a Remington 9 mm laid on the floor under it. "Who found him?" I asked.

"His wife heard the gunshot and came running downstairs. I'm afraid she's pretty shook up. The doctor has already been here and given her a sedative. She's asleep upstairs. The doc called a nurse to stay tonight, and we'll control the crime scene. Tomorrow she needs to find somewhere else to stay. Mary too." John said.

"I knew he was having a tough time, but I never thought he would do this." I murmured more to myself than John. I was devastated. I had known Roy for over thirty-five years. He wasn't just a political ally, he was a friend. We played golf, dined, drank and vacationed. Why didn't he come to me?

"It's a little too early to call it suicide. The detectives will be doing a thorough investigation. I'll keep you in the loop, I promise." He volunteered.

"Think it would be ok if I looked in on Sarah?" I asked.

"I don't know if she'll know you're there, but sure. Doc says she'll probably sleep through the night." John said.

I went upstairs to see Sarah. The nurse was sitting next to her bed reading, and rose to give me her seat. "Sarah, its Don." There was no movement or acknowledgement by Sarah. "When she wakes, let her know I'll be back in the morning."

"I'm afraid she's sedated so she probably won't come around until morning. You can leave her a note if you like," said the nurse. She handed me paper and pen and I left Sarah a quick note saying I would be return in the morning.

"John, will they seal off the library since it's a crime scene? I wouldn't want Sarah to come down and revisit the library," I inquired

"You don't have to worry, Don. There'll be three officers in the house and another unit outside. The library will remain sealed so we preserve the scene until the detectives release it. I'm still not comfortable that this was a suicide, so I want to make sure Sarah is safe." John said.

"Thanks, John, I'll be back in the morning to see Sarah and if there's anything else I can do, let me know." I volunteered.

As soon as I got home, I called Tony. "Tony, Don Leslie, I just left Roy Drucker's house. Apparently, he shot himself this evening. I'm sure it will be in the morning news. I knew the pressure was getting to him with the election only a week away, and the pressure from Amanda always wanting comments from him. I should have paid more attention." I said

"Don, you can't blame yourself for this. Roy was an adult. He knew what the stakes were. I'm really sorry he couldn't handle the pressure, but this is not on you. I'm going to have to talk with the Company about our next move, and I'll let you know what they advise. Is there anything we can do for the widow? Tony asked.

"I don't know what the funeral arrangements might be, or her financial condition, but I'm going back tomorrow to talk to Sarah. The doc has her sedated. She found the body and it was not a pretty scene." I replied. "It will be all over the papers tomorrow."

"Let me know how things are going, or if the widow needs anything. We take care of our friends. I'll let you know what the Company has to say." Tony explained.

As usual with Tony, it's less about what he says than how he says it. I had that feeling in the pit of my stomach, you know when something just doesn't seem right. I tried hard to ignore it. I was exhausted. I needed to try to sleep so I could be fresh when I got back to Drucker's house in the morning.

Chapter 12

The House Loses

Mayor Drucker's House

Morning arrived right on schedule despite the fact I had only two hours of fitful sleep. I hurriedly dressed and headed for Sarah's. I didn't want her to wake and not find a friendly face, especially now.

There was a unit stationed outside the house, in an unmarked vehicle. "Hey fellas, I thought you might need some coffee." I said as I handed coffees to the two cops. They were appreciative. Babysitting was boring work for policemen.

I entered the double mahogany doors of the house and was greeted by one of the policeman stationed at the door of the library. The detectives were in the library reviewing the crime scene.

"Don," detective Stanley said as he walked out of the library. "We wanted to talk with the widow, but she insisted on waiting for you."

"I'll go up and get her. We'll be down shortly," I said. "Make sure the doors to the library are closed, please." My legs felt like lead and each step of the grand staircase was a struggle. I'm thinking the whole time, what could say to a woman who found her husband's brains splattered all over the leaded glass windows. I reached the bedroom far too soon, took a deep breath, and knocked. "Sarah?" I inquired.

The door flew open and she was sobbing in my arms before I could say another word. "I don't understand, Don. Roy would never do…what they said he did. We're Catholic. He just wouldn't." She half cried.

"I know, Sarah. The detectives will get to the bottom of this. They have a few questions to ask you. Let's go downstairs. I'll stay with you. It's just routine." I explained as I lead her down the stairway.

"Detective Stanley, let's go to the living room." I directed as I guided Sarah to the overstuffed sofa. Sarah, you don't have to answer any question if you don't want to. The detectives are just trying to find out what happened." I explained, with a protective arm still around Sarah.

"No. I want to tell you everything. You have to find who did this. My husband would never commit suicide." She insisted rather defiantly.

"That's why we're investigating, Mrs. Drucker. We want to be sure exactly what happened. We don't take anything at face value, I assure you." He said. "Can you tell us about your evening?"

I could feel Sarah shaking, still sitting with my protective arm around her. "Well, he got home a little later than usual, around seven o'clock. He didn't want dinner. He insisted he just needed some alone time. I was a little miffed because I made his favorite, pot roast. Then he went in the library. Oh, and he said no phone calls no matter who it was. Then he went in the library and closed the doors." She explained.

"Was that the last time you saw him?" Asked Detective Stanley.

"Well yes, but I knocked on the door just before I went to bed to see if he wanted coffee. He yelled no, and I told him I was going to bed. It was ten o'clock." She explained.

"And how sure are you of the exact time," Asked Detective Stanley.

"I think it's very important for your health to maintain a consistent schedule. I always go to bed at ten o'clock and rise at seven o'clock. Last night I went to bed at ten o'clock as always." She said.

"What happened next? He inquired.

"I awoke from a sound sleep by a loud bang. I went downstairs and knocked on the library door. When there was no answer, I opened the door. I think I must have screamed because Mary, our maid, came running." Her voice had gotten shakier as she spoke.

"I think that's about enough for today, detectives." I said.

"We're almost done. Mrs. Drucker tell us what happened next."

"I don't really…I'm not sure. I think Mary took me out of the room and called the police. It's kind of a blur. I'm sorry detective, I just….." she trailed off. Now she went from sobbing to a full cry.

"That's it, we're done. Why don't we get some coffee, Sarah? Detective, I think we need a little break." I said.

"We'll interview the maid next. Will you send her in on your way out?" He asked.

I took Sarah into the kitchen and sent Mary in to Detective Stanley. I sat Sarah down at the kitchen table with a cup of black coffee. She looked so lost. The sun was streaming in the leaded glass window by the table, and the bright sun on the bevels caused tiny colors to dance across the floor. I thought the sun had no respect for what happened. It should have been a gray, overcast, depressing day, but the sun refused to cooperate. If it wasn't for the half dead plants, it could have had the appearance of a summer day. Sarah took another sip and I joined her.

****

"Mary, what is your relationship to the Drucker family? Asked the detective.

"I moved into this house with Miss Sarah's parents, right after the house was built. I have a two-room suite upstairs. I maintained the house, and took care of Miss Sarah. When they died, I stayed on and Miss Sarah and Roy moved back into the house." Mary explained.

"Tell me what happened last night," asked the detective.

"Well, I went to bed not long after Miss Sarah. I read for a short while and then fell asleep. There was a loud noise that woke me, and then I heard Miss Sarah scream. I went running down the stairs and found her standing at the library door screaming again and again. I grabbed her by her shoulders and took her to the living room. I sat her on the couch and then called the police. Then I went back to Miss Sarah and stayed with her until the police arrived." Explained Mary.

"Did you at any time go into the library and check on Mr. Drucker?" Asked the detective.

"No. Never."

Just then the doorbell rang. “Excuse me, sir. I need to get that.” Mary said. She answered the door and showed the gentleman to the kitchen, and then rejoined the detective in the living room.

****

“Don, Sarah, I am so sorry to hear about Roy.” Offered Bill. Bill was the local funeral director, and was well-known to anyone important in Terre Haute. He sat down at the table and held Sarah’s hand. “I came by to express my sympathy for your loss.” He continued to hold Sarah’s hand as he spoke. He had a soft, reassuring voice that helped melt away some of the tension surrounding death. “Mind if I help myself to a cup of that coffee?”

Sarah automatically started to get up to get him coffee. “No dear, I’ll get it. Just relax.”

Bill came back to the table and the three of us preceded to tell our favorite Roy story. It was comforting to share Roy’s special qualities with people who also had a deep respect for him. Bill managed to diplomatically get to the point of his visit.

"I'm not allowed to say who, but someone has come forward and wants to make sure Roy gets a funeral worthy of a beloved man." Bill said.

"Don, did you do this?" Sarah asked.

"No Sarah. I would have if needed, but someone beat me to it." I got up to get another cup of coffee, and watched as Bill and Sarah worked out the details of the funeral. I knew damn well who was paying for this public display of affection. I remembered Tony's words about taking care of family. Obviously, Tony had spared no expense. I don't think Bill had ever had the opportunity to pull out all the stops; budgets usually limited what he could do. Evidently budget was of no concern to Roy's benefactor. This was going to be a true black tie event. Roy would have appreciated that.

I half listened from my seat at the kitchen island. I heard the antique hearse, and flowers from Heather, a supremely talented local florist. There was to be a two hour visitation at the funeral home, making it more comfortable for those who were afraid God might strike them dead if they entered a church. Most of Roy's friends and business partners would fall into that category. Then they would proceed to St. Mary's Catholic Church where there would be high mass normally reserved for dignitaries. I pictured Roy sitting on a cloud, sipping his scotch and soda, and offering his suggestions to the already over-blown affair.

"Don, I assume you will do the eulogy before Father Murdock begins the mass. I think Roy would have wanted that," said Bill. His suggestion shook me out of my haze.

"Oh Don, please, I wouldn't trust anyone else. Roy would have wanted you." Sarah implored.

"Of course I will." I'll bet Roy nearly fell off his cloud laughing at this turn of events. I could see him toasting to my misery. Yeah, I'm sure he was enjoying every minute of this.

Bill and Sarah finished their arrangements, and Bill gave Sarah's hand a squeeze. "Don, I'll keep in touch," he said and shook my hand.

The detectives had finished with Mary and she joined us in the kitchen. "Sarah, can I fix you some breakfast. You have to eat," she insisted.

"No, nothing Mary." Sarah replied

"Sarah, you can't stay here until after they finish their investigation. Why don't you and Mary pack some bags, and I'll take you to the Terre Haute

House. They should be done here in a few days. Go grab some clothes and such while I step outside for a smoke." She went upstairs with Mary close behind, and I went outside. As soon as I opened the door, I was bombarded by reporters screaming questions from across the driveway. The police unit assigned had been joined by two additional units, and they had set up a perimeter across the driveway.

The young police officer from the original unit came up the stairs. "We're keeping them away from the house, but they are eager for any information."

"It's ok. I'm taking Mary and Mrs. Drucker to the Terre Haute House. They're getting their stuff together now. I'll go say a few words to the reporters. Will you make sure they don't come outside till I'm back?" I asked and headed off toward the noisy group on the lawn.

"I'd like to make a brief comment. My long-time associate and a great friend to the city of Terre Haute died last night. The police are investigating, and I'm sure they will make information available to you as soon as possible." I said.

Questions flew quickly: "Is it true he took his own life? Do you think the election had something to do with his death? "Was there any sign of foul play?" Yada, yada, yada. I ignored them all and returned to the house. When I entered, Sarah, Mary, and our helpful young policeman were coming down the stairway to the foyer. He excused himself to put the bags in my car.

"Now ladies, the front lawn is full of reporters. I've already given them a statement. We're going to go out the door, get in the car, and leave as quickly as possible. I don't want anyone following us." I said.

The police did a great job delaying all the vehicles long enough for us to get an ample lead. I'm pretty sure they would anticipate Sarah staying at the Terre Haute House, the local upscale hotel. We arrived without a tail and entered from the back. Jack Long, manager of the Terre Haute House, met us and took us directly to the presidential suite.

"If you need anything, just call 568. The kitchen is open twenty four hours a day for room service. We'll give you your privacy. If you have any questions, call the front desk. They'll get me. Again, let me say I am so sorry for your loss, and we will try to make your stay as comfortable as possible," explained Mr. Long.

"Thanks Jack. I appreciate your discretion," I said as Jack left. I'm going to give you ladies time to unpack and get settled. If you need anything, call me Sarah."

"Don't worry Mr. Don, I'll take care of Miss Sarah", Mary volunteered.

"I know you will, Mary. Thanks."

As soon as I got to the office, I called Tony. "Tony, Don Leslie, I just wanted to thank you for paying all the funeral expenses for Roy."

"I told you Don, we take care of our own." He said. "Is Sarah all right with Bill taking care of the details? I told Bill to go first class all the way."

"I think Sarah was relieved, both emotionally and financially, that someone else was handling everything." I said.

"Good."

"I'm a pall bearer, and Bill asked me to give the eulogy at the church service. The cops haven't ruled Roy's death a suicide yet. You don't think Chicago could have a hand in Roy's death, do you?" I asked.

"I don't think so, Don. I know they are heavily backing Johnson because they really want Terre Haute, but I don't think Roy was a threat to them." Tony said. "Let me know if there's anything else I can do."

I had an uneasy feeling as I hung up from Tony. I decided to call Sheriff Wesley and see where the investigation stood.

Chapter 13

The Usual Suspects

I gave Sheriff Wesley a call as soon as I hung up from Tony. "John, how about dinner tonight? Maybe you can catch me up on Roy's investigation." I asked.

"Actually, I was getting ready to call you." He replied. "Shall we meet at The Pick? Seven o'clock?"

"Sure. See you then."

I was surprised when I entered the private dining room at the Pick to see, not just John, but the police chief and the two detectives on the case. There was a fifth man I didn't recognize.

"Don you know everyone but Reggie," who stood and offered his hand. "Reggie is the head pathologist with the Crime Investigation Unit. He has pertinent information for us." John said.

We all ordered food and drink, and made small talk until the waitress served us.

"Make sure we're not interrupted John directed to the waitress. I'm going to let Reggie bring you up to date on the forensic evidence."

"Thanks, John. There were two bullets that entered the skull of Mr. Drucker. They were so close together, it was not immediately apparent there was a second bullet. People who shoot themselves generally shoot themselves in the temple. It would be terribly difficult to shoot yourself in the forehead, and obviously, it would be impossible to shoot the gun twice. Based on the lack of powder burns and the trajectory of the bullet, the gun was approximately six feet away, and was fired at a forty-five degree angle. That would mean that someone standing on the other side of his desk would have been in a perfect position to shoot Mr.

Drucker. I will officially rule his death a homicide." Reggie explained.

"Also, there was no sign of forced entry so whoever was there Roy didn't think posed a threat. I thought you should hear the report before it hits the paper tomorrow. Obviously the detectives will have more questions for Mrs. Drucker." John said.

"You can't think for a moment that Sarah had anything to do with his death!" I exclaimed.

"No certainly not," replied Detective Stanley. "I have a pretty good gut about these things, but I think she may be able to tell us who might have had a grudge with the Mayor. A lot of times people know things that seem inconsequential to them, but can give us a direction that proves to be fruitful. I'm hoping further conversation can point us in a new direction. Think you can get Sarah to help us out?"

"Absolutely, I'll talk to Sarah after the funeral tomorrow. I'm sure tomorrow will be out of the question, but how about ten o'clock at the Terre Haute House the next day. I think she would be more comfortable if I'm there, is that ok? I asked.

"Sure Don, that's fine." Said Stanley. "I don't suppose you have any ideas that might help us out?"

"Well, I can tell you what you've heard on the news about the Chicago connection is true. They are behind Johnson's run for Mayor. Maybe they thought Johnson wasn't going to win, so they decided to assure his victory by eliminating the competition." I offered.

"We've actually been looking into that already. Do you have any specific people in mind? Chicago is a big outfit. It sure would help if we could narrow it down to five or six individuals." He asked.

"Sorry, I'm not aware of the specifics of their involvement, other than what's been reported, but maybe that news reporter, Amanda, could help you out." I suggested. It would be nice to see the media being hounded for a change.

"She's on our list to be interviewed," Stanley said. "Reporters tend to be less than forthcoming with their sources, but we are going to see what we can get from her."

"I'll put out some feelers, too, and see if anyone has an idea where this might have come from or who might have the authority to order a hit on a mayor. Killing a mayor is going to attract a lot of attention; not generally something Chicago would welcome." I said.

“I’d appreciate anything you can do for us, Don.”

I knew without a doubt Chicago was behind this. As soon as we concluded our business, I called Tony. “Tony, Don Leslie. How are things in Vegas?”

“Good Don. How are things going there? Everything set for tomorrow? He asked.

“I talked with Bill Gooding today. Showing at the funeral home will be nine until eleven, then off to St. Mary’s for the mass at noon. Burial at the cemetery will follow. It promises to be the show of a lifetime. I’m sure Roy would appreciate it. Thanks again for making that happen.” I said.

“I assume you’ll be with Sarah the whole time?

“Yes, of course, and Mary will be with her as well. Tony, I called for another reason. I talked with the police pathologist last night. They are going to rule Roy’s death a homicide. It will, undoubtedly hit the papers tomorrow. Would Chicago have ordered a hit on the Mayor?” I asked.

“They wouldn’t have ordered a hit without talking to me, and no one mentioned anything,” Tony replied.

Although he said no, I just couldn't dismiss the nagging feeling that he was well aware of what had happened to Roy. Maybe he even had a hand in it. "Well, I wanted to keep you informed of the latest developments. I have a big day tomorrow, so I'm going to bed. I'm sure we'll talk again." My stomach was churning as I went over the day's events. I had to get focused on Roy's eulogy. I went to the office and sat looking at the blank page, trying to sum up Roy in ten minutes or less. I poured myself a bourbon, and toasted to Roy. I felt Roy's presence, envisioning him in the leather chair across from me, drinking his scotch and soda as he had so many times before. Help me out here buddy, I said out loud to his empty chair. I reflected on our long association. He was a business associate with his hand in my pocket like so many others, but he was more than that. He was a kindred spirit, a friend, and a man to admire for his tenacity. He could have become a poor victim at twelve and ended up just another underachiever trying to keep his head above water, while raising a family. Instead, he rose above his humble beginnings and ruled over Terre Haute like a compassionate dictator. Although he collected his share of kickbacks, he always had the city in his heart. He loved Terre Haute like a child loves a shiny new toy on Christmas morn. It truly did belong to him, and

Terre Haute was going to miss him. I raised the glass to his empty chair, and began to write.

****

Sarah and Mary were having coffee and toast when I arrived. Had it not been for the fact that their dresses were black, they could have been going to a party. Each wore a hat and had their gloves. I grabbed a cup of coffee and sat down.

"How are you ladies this morning?

"I'm doing ok. Mary has been great. I can't tell you how much I appreciate staying here. I don't think I could go back to the house right now." She said.

"There's something I have to tell you, Sarah. I had a meeting last night with the detectives and a guy from the Criminal Investigation Unit. They are ruling Roy's death a homicide," I said. I expected her to be relieved, but she was elated.

"I knew he would never commit suicide. I tried to tell them that." She was pleased to be vindicated.

"They're going to want to talk to both of us again to see if we can shed light on anyone who might have an axe to grind with Roy. I told them we would meet here at the hotel tomorrow at ten. Is that ok with you?" I asked.

"Absolutely. I want to find out who did this and see the bastard punished," she said in an extraordinarily angry way. The usual mild-mannered Sarah was eager for retribution, a side I had fortunately never seen before.

Having finished their toast and coffee, the ladies donned their mink coats and we left for the funeral home. When we arrived, Bill greeted us at the door, and after securing our coats, showed us into the parlor. There was not a surface anywhere that was not covered with a flower arrangement. The casket spray was magnificent, combining dried and fresh flowers in a blaze of color. It dripped over the side of the blue metal casket, and weaved into the spray was a red ribbon with words "The Heart of Terre Haute". We took our time looking at each and every arrangement. There were flowers from the city departments and various golfing and poker buddies as expected, but surprisingly, there were also lots of flowers sent by citizens that Roy had touched in one way or another. The sweet smell of the assembled floral displays was almost overwhelming. Extra tables had been brought in to contain the more than usual number of flowers. Larger arrangements and tall plants were in front near the casket. Bill had collected pictures previously displayed in Roy's office and arranged them on a large bulletin board. There were pictures of Roy with visiting dignitaries from JFK to Elvis. The range of people Roy knew and appreciated were far reaching. Sarah was completely overwhelmed by the sight.

I always hate it when people say a dead person looks so natural….they're dead. I have to say though Bill had done a marvelous job on Roy, even though most of the back of his head had been missing. He looked like he could have climbed right out of the casket and joined me for a drink. Sarah was quite complimentary. She and Bill talked quietly while I roamed the room looking for a specific arrangement. I found it. A very large arrangement with star gaze lilies and snap dragons. "Sorry for your loss, Tony Collota."

"We'll collect all the flowers and cards for you. Part of the flowers will go to the church with Roy, and we'll send part of them to the graveside. There will still be many, many left. Green plants will, of course, be delivered to your house along with any specific floral arrangements you want. If you need help writing cards, we can have someone help you with that. You just let us know what you need," Bill said.

"Can the extra flowers go to the nursing homes? I can't possibly take all these." Sarah suggested.

"We can take care of that for you. We'll be taking Roy to the church in the 1921 LaSalle hearse. He always appreciated a good ride," Bill said and smiled.

"I'll give you a little privacy before we open for the viewing. Don, when you're ready, just open the door to the parlor. Take as long as you need," he said and then left to direct people who were already arriving.

"Sarah, I'll be right here with you," Mary said. When the ladies were ready, they positioned themselves by the casket and the Knights of Columbus took their guard positions on either side of the casket. It was quite an impressive display. When I opened the parlor door, the lobby outside the parlor was already overflowing. I stepped out to greet people in line. The parade of people was steady until eleven, when Bill explained to those left that we would be moving to St. Mary's Church for services.

I had never been in St. Mary's before. It is one of the oldest Catholic churches in Terre Haute. It was built at a time when opulence and craftsmanship were celebrated. All the wood in the church was carved with gothic arches and topped with spires. The ceiling was hand-painted wood with subdued colors of greens, browns, and oranges. There was a gigantic gold organ that dominated one side of the altar. The priest's pulpit topped a small circular stairway, and hung out toward the pews. There was a small podium in front of the organ used by ordinary folks participating in the service. Behind the altar was an ivory colored crucifix with a fifteen foot tall Jesus. Stained glass windows lined either side of the church and depicted the Stations of the Cross. The sun shone through them, splashing the church with jewel toned colors. Every seat was full, including the balcony. I think most of Terre Haute was there. The priest, in his formal robes, led the casket with Mom, Sarah and me following. He ascended to the pulpit and the three of us took the front row seats.

There were some preliminary comments from the priest, none of which I can remember. At the appropriate time, he introduced me to those assembled, and I found myself standing behind the podium. I kept his eulogy proper and befitting the Catholic audience I was addressing. His inner circle had planned a wake for tonight at The Pick. We left the church and followed the old hearse to the cemetery with about fifty other cars. Being a veteran of the Great War, Roy received full military honors at the gravesite. I am always impressed with the dignity and serious dedication the Honor Guard shows. I took Mary and Sarah back to the hotel, and we had a small dinner.

Roy's inner circle of friends, that is to say his golfing, drinking, gambling and eating buddies, were to meet at The Pick at seven that evening. The large conference room capable of seating one hundred people, easily held the hundred and fifty people that came and went throughout the evening. There were three cash bars and bar-top tables set up throughout the room. Small groups would congregate around a table, there would be a Roy story shared, and the group would toast and roar with laughter. This was repeated over and over. I stayed until there were only five of us left. We made a final toast to Roy's safe journey to the other side, and left with stories of Roy's humanity in our hearts and heads.

Tomorrow was the interview with the detectives, and I was not looking forward to that. I had already told the detectives about the Chicago connection to the campaign money, which was now public knowledge anyway. I DID NOT mention it was Tony who set up that whole scam.

Chapter 14

Hide and Seek

Mayor Drucker's Library

We were just finishing breakfast in the suite when the detectives arrived. They were right on time. We moved to the living room and Mary offered the detectives coffee which they gladly accepted.

"Sarah, I am so sorry to have to do this now, but we're trying to narrow down suspects as soon as possible. Did Roy ever get any phone calls at home that made him uneasy?" asked Detective Stanley.

"He would get a phone call, and if it was business related, he would take it in his library so I never heard many of his conversations. One time he did get a call during dinner and he took it in the foyer," she said.

"Can you remember anything about that conversation?" he asked.

"Yes. He seemed quite upset that this person had called our home. He said, "Don't call me again", and then, "let's see what Tony thinks about that. I think that was the name," Sarah explained.

"That's great, Sarah," said the detective as he sat forward in his chair, seemingly encouraged by this tidbit.

"I recall," she paused, "Don, you know a Tony don't you?"

"I do know a guy in Vegas named Tony," I said. "Roy and I went out there a couple weeks back for a long weekend. He comped our rooms."

"How well do you know this Tony?" Asked the detective.

"I wrote a bail bond on him about four or five years ago. He told me if I ever came to Vegas, he'd comp our room. I didn't really know if he would, but I gave him a call and he did. Turns out he runs the Flamingo," I said. I tried to act like this was just a usual Vegas kind of deal. I didn't mention it was the Executive Suite or that he included all our meals and entertainment. I told him just enough so he wouldn't be suspicious.

"Can either of you think of anyone else?" asked detective Stanley.

"I'm sure Roy had a hate mail folder. I assume you've gone through that group?" I suggested.

"We have guys checking those right now. We're also checking anyone involved in a lawsuit with the city who might have an axe to grind," Detective Stanley chimed in.

"Sounds to me like you've got an extensive list of possible suspects. You can't really be Mayor as long as Roy, and not develop a huge following of lovers and haters. " I said. "Sounds like you've got your hands full."

"This mystery man on the phone, any idea why Roy would have a concern about this man?" asked Detective Stanley.

"I don't think we would be talking about the same Tony as the guy in Vegas. There must be a local guy named Tony." I was again trying to lead them away from our Vegas connection.

"Do you have a safe in the house?" asked the detective. "Sometimes there's paperwork that can give us clues to some of his business partners that might be unknown to you."

"Yes, there's a wall safe in the library," replied Sarah.

"May we have permission to open that safe? Do you have the combination for it?" Asked Detective Stanley.

"Of course. It is behind the hunt picture in the library. I'll write down the combination. There is also a box that Roy said I should have if anything ever happened to him. I totally forgot about it," she said.

"Where would we find this box, Mrs. Drucker?" asked the detective.

"It should be on the top shelf of my clothes closet. It's pink with roses on it."

"Is there any other place Roy might have put important papers?" I asked.

"There would be papers in his desk and there is a filing cabinet in the library. Do you know when I can go home, detective?" she asked.

"The crime scene clean up should be finished in the next two days, and then you can go back. Do you happen to have a spare key for your house?" asked detective Stanley.

"You can have mine, detective," I offered.

"I think that's all for now, Mrs. Drucker. I appreciate you giving us the time to talk to you. Again, let me say how sorry I am for your loss. Roy was loved by a great many people, and we're all going to feel the loss," said the detective.

"I'll walk you fellows out," I said as we all got up to leave. "I'm going to the office girls. I'll see you tonight for dinner." I followed the detectives outside.

"Don, we have a warrant to search the house, but I wanted to try to get Sarah's consent without upsetting her. We'll do the search ourselves, and we'll be extremely careful to disturb as little as possible."

"I assumed you would be searching the house once it was declared a homicide, but I do appreciate your diplomatic approach with Sarah. I know you'll be respectful while you're searching. Thanks fellas," I said as I shook both their hands.

I have to say I was more than a little nervous about what the good detectives might find buried in Roy's paperwork, but I'd have to deal with whatever they found. This wasn't going to go away.

Detective Stanley was true to his word. He was gentle with all of the Drucker's possessions. They started with the safe, thinking valuable assets would be kept there. Just as Sarah had said, there was a small safe in the wall tucked behind the oil painting of a hunt scene. Anticipating scandalous papers and a private stash of money, they were disappointed to find the safe totally empty.

Their next great hope was the box that Roy said Sarah should review when he died. It was easily located just where Sarah said it would be. Taking it down from the closet shelf, they hoped it would offer some clues to his murder.

“I’ll go through the box, you start with the library desk. Be sure to check for false bottoms or secret panels in the antique desk. Old desks frequently had such things, and those would be great hiding places,” detective Stanley ordered Kenney.

Detective Stanley started taking things out of the box. Surprisingly, there was a stack of old letters from Sarah, tied with a ribbon. Who knew Roy was such an old softie! There was a hundred thousand dollar life insurance policy with me listed as the contact person. I remember selling Roy that policy early in my life insurance career. There were deeds to several rental properties and his house. The funeral arrangements had been spelled out for Sarah, although it was too late for that.

The rest of the search proved even less exciting. There were papers put in various drawers which they boxed up to review later. They also found several bank statements from at least three different accounts. After reviewing them they discovered one was his rental property account, one his personal checking, and one his personal savings. After reviewing the activity, they found nothing suspicious in any of them.

They found nothing which would indicate a person with a grudge who might want Roy dead. I was pretty sure that would be the case. Roy always had a fatherly approach to everyone. He cared about the citizens and the city. I can't imagine anyone hating him enough to kill him. So back to square one.

I called Tony after talking to Stanley about what they had found. "Tony, Don Leslie."

"Hey, Don. How was the funeral?" Tony asked.

"Roy would have been impressed. I think everyone in Terre Haute was there, and Bill really pulled out all the stops. He used the old LaSalle hearse. There were so many flowers, there was hardly room for people. The church was magnificent, and packed to the rafters. Sarah was definitely not up to dealing with funeral planning and payment. You really lessened her load, and I totally appreciate that." I said.

"We have to take care of our own, you know. How is the investigation going?" Tony asked.

"They searched Roy's house, but didn't find anything of use. No surprises there. They also searched the office, but nothing there either. Last I heard they were checking out lawsuits against the city to see if anything panned out there. I know they canvassed the neighborhood but didn't find any witnesses. I'm getting the feeling they're at a dead end." I said. "There are a lot of people wanting to find out what bastard did this."

"I'm glad nothing incriminating turned up to mess with your situation. Have you heard anything from Chicago?" Tony asked.

"No, just that one call. How about you? Have they contacted you?" I asked.

"They're always in contact with us. I haven't been told what is going to happen now. I did tell them they had ruled Roy's death a homicide, but I didn't get any kind of rise out of them. I honestly don't think they had anything to do with his death. They would have clued me in if they did." Tony said.

"I'm still not convinced, but I'll take your word for it."

"Believe me, Don, if Chicago had wanted to make his death look like a suicide, they would have done a perfect job. No one would ever have suspected he was murdered. This was a pretty sloppy job. I think you're looking at a local problem. If you want some help working on this, I can send Mr. Smith over for a week or so. Just let me know." Tony offered.

"I think we're good right now, but if things start stalling, I might reconsider that offer. Thanks Tony," I said.

I had barely hung up from Tony, when Detective Stanley called me. "Hey Don, I thought I'd let you know that the cleanup crew is done with the crime scene so Sarah and Mary can go home anytime they want. I checked it out myself when they finished, and there is absolutely no evidence of what happened in the library. I told the cops I left at the house that when you get there, they can leave."

"I'll talk to Sarah tonight and see when she wants to go back home. She's been pretty anxious to get back there. "Thanks again, detective, for the consideration you showed Sarah. It's really appreciated. If I can do anything for you, just call me." I said.

I called Sarah as soon as I hung up from Detective Stanley. "Sarah, I just got off the phone with detective Stanley, and he says you can go home any time you want."

"Don, I can't tell you how much I have appreciated staying at the hotel, but I so want to go home," she said as her voice waivered a little. "When do you think we can go?"

"Actually, I'm pretty free of appointments this afternoon so any time you want to go would be fine." I offered.

"I can be packed up by the time you get here," she said.

"I'm on my way. See you soon." When I arrived at the hotel, Sarah and Mary were ready to go. We managed to leave from the back door without attracting any attention.

As we drove up the driveway, Sarah seemed to lose some of her initial enthusiasm for returning home. She held tightly to Mary's hand as she exited the car. I followed with the bags.

Sarah immediately went to the library doors, but stopped short of entering the library. "It's ok Miss Sarah," said Mary as she opened the doors.

I was surprised at the excellent job the crime clean-up unit had done on the library. There was nothing out of place, despite the detectives search, and there was not an inkling of the previous violence. The stained glass windows, previously dulled by Roy's brain matter, now gleamed in the sunlight. Sarah walked around the library with Mary close by.

"Miss Sarah, why don't we go to the kitchen and I'll make us some coffee. I have some cinnamon coffee cake," Mary said, gently directing her toward the door of the kitchen.

"I'll put your bags upstairs, Sarah." I said.

When I returned Sarah was sitting in the large bay window which contained the breakfast table. Mary was at the island plating the warm coffee cake. The windows surrounding the bay were devoid of curtains allowing the sun to stream in making the kitchen bright and cheery. After bringing us all coffee and cake, Mary sat down at the table with us.

Sarah reached across the table and patted Mary's hand. "I don't know what I would do without you, Mary."

"You know, I'll always be here for you Miss Sarah," replied Mary.

They shared a special bond. Mary had been with Sarah's parents in this same house. I guessed she was about sixty. Considering she worked inside and outside the house every day, she was in excellent health. She could easily pass for fifty. When Sarah's parents died, Sarah and Roy moved in and Mary stayed. She loved the family, and it was great knowing that Mary was there for Sarah, especially now. We ate our coffee cake and sipped coffee while discussing what a beautiful day it was. It was spring in Indiana. That time when it was seventy and sunny one day, and forty and rainy the next. There was always a struggle between winter and spring. Eventually spring would prevail, but not without an argument with winter. I left when Sarah and Mary started discussing a retail therapy trip. Sarah was in good hands.

Chapter 15

Not Bad for a Dead Guy

The local power brokers met at The Pick to watch the election results. Even though Roy was dead, it was too late to remove him from the ballots or find an alternative candidate, so the election went forward as planned.

Sheriff Wesley, Prosecutor Wiseman, the Chief, as well as Judge Stevens and Harmon joined me for dinner in the private dining room at The Pick. We planned for a long evening. "This is bizarre to sit here and watch an election for a dead man," said Wesley.

"Somehow I think Roy would appreciate the irony. Let's toast to Roy and wish him good luck in the election," Wiseman suggested.

"I agree. To Roy," I said as I raised my glass.

We polished off dinner by eight as the first results were starting to roll in. Roy was leading with seventy percent of the votes in. It's a testament to Roy's record that even dead, he was a better candidate than Johnson. We continued to drink and toast Roy with each updated report. Finally, about ten o'clock they called the race. Johnson managed to win the election by twenty-six votes. Normally there would be a recount but with Roy gone, that wouldn't happen.

"Well, I think Roy made a fantastic showing. He should be proud", said the Chief. We toasted Roy one last time and the party broke up about midnight.

I kept thinking about Roy on the way home, and who could have such hatred for him. I still came back to Chicago, and I thought Tony knew far more than he was sharing. I decided to call Tony tomorrow after a good night's sleep. Right now I just needed to go to bed.

The next afternoon I called Tony. "Hey Don, I heard Roy nearly beat out Johnson. That would really have been something. A dead candidate winning an election. Talk about embarrassing."

"If Roy were alive, we'd be waiting on a recount right now. Twenty-six votes. That's all Johnson had over Roy. Roy would have had his eighth consecutive term as mayor. What a testament to him." I was proud of Roy's performance, although I had nothing to do with it.

"Tony, the investigation has suddenly stalled, and I'm wondering if you've heard anything about it from the Chicago Company," I said.

"I'm telling you, Don, Chicago had nothing to do with Roy's death. If they had, I would have known," Tony argued.

I still wasn't convinced that Chicago didn't have a hand in his death, but there was no proof that they did. After I talked with Tony, I decided to drop by and see how Sarah was doing. Having no children of their own, and both Sarah and Roy being only children, meant there was no family for Sarah to rely upon. Mary was the closest thing to family Sarah had. I was sure Sarah could use a little company so I swung by to check on her.

Mary greeted me at the front door and took me to the kitchen. I sat down at the breakfast table and she had coffee in front of me immediately. "Miss Sarah will be down shortly. She's finishing up some thank you notes."

"Mary, how long have you been with this family?" I asked.

"I was eighteen when I started to work for Miss Sarah's parents. They had just finished the grand house. I cooked and cleaned and took care of Miss Sarah. When they died, Miss Sarah inherited the house and me. I still cook and clean and take care of Miss Sarah," said Mary. "This is the only home I've ever had. Mr. Don, can I speak freely to you?"

"Of course."

Mary sat down at the table and proceeded to speak in a very quiet voice. "Mr. Don, I've seen a lot of things in this house. Things people don't know anything about. I've held Miss Sarah crying in my arms too many times after Mr. Roy knocked her around. If you ask me, it was about time someone knocked him around. I say good riddance to a real bad egg." The hatred she had for Roy was obvious as she spoke about him. It took me by surprise. Since we usually met at a bar or restaurant, I had only been to Roy's house twice in all the time I knew him, but I had no idea there were any problems between Sarah and Roy. "Everybody loved Mr. Roy, but I tell you he was mean to Miss Sarah. I should have killed him myself. With that, she got up and crossed the room to a door which opened onto a servant's stairway.

Mary disappeared up the stairway, and was back in the kitchen nearly immediately. "Miss Sarah will be right down," she said.

"Thanks." I said. I began to feel a knot in my stomach as I started putting the pieces together. The police had assumed Roy let his killer in and then invited him to join him in the library long after Sarah went to bed. He therefore, must have known and trusted his killer.

I sat at the table and stared at the doorway to the back stairway. I ran through the scenario in my mind. She could have easily gotten Roy's gun, come down the servant's stairs, shot him, and back up in time to run down the main stairway and find

Sarah at the library door. *It wasn't Chicago that killed Roy; it was Mary. Right under the nose of the Terre Haute Police Dept. and me, this sixty-year-old woman managed to kill the mayor and get away with it!* I guess I owed Tony an apology. Chicago really didn't have anything to do with Roy's murder.

Sarah came into the kitchen and startled me out of my musing. "Good morning, Don. Is Mary taking good care of you?" said Sarah.

"Absolutely. Her homemade coffee cake is the best. How are you this morning?" I asked Sarah.

"Actually, I'm doing pretty well. Mary's been a real help. I don't know what I would do without her. She's always been there for me, since I was a little girl." said Sarah. "I'm so sorry about your Mom, Don. I wish I had known her better."

"She was one of a kind. I never heard her talk badly about anyone, ever. It's been a rough few months. Losing my Mom and then Roy." My voice trailed off as I spoke, and I fought to hold back tears.

"Believe me, Don, I know how it feels. I never thought I would be alone at this time in my life. If there is anything I can do, please, please tell me," she said.

"I'm glad you're doing so well, Sarah. I just dropped by to see if you need any help."

"I'm feeling much better. I'm sleeping better, and I'm relaxing and letting Mary spoil me. I didn't realize how tense things had gotten between Roy and me. I feel a little guilty because I'm almost relieved," she confided.

"I can see everything is going well here. I'm meeting with the guys at The Pick later for dinner so I need to get going. If you need anything all you have to do is call me." I said as I got up to leave.

Chapter 16

Going Legit

Driving to The Pick later that evening, I again found myself thinking about Mary and Roy. How could I have missed all the signs? Like a homeless person you tend to walk past without notice, Mary just blended in with the house. Should I say something to Sheriff Wesley? Sarah seemed almost happy, and certainly Mary would continue to take good care of her. I argued with myself all the way to The Pick. I ultimately decided I had no proof of anything, and Sarah seemed happier than I had seen her in years. If the police found out, they would have to do it without my help.

And then there was Mom. I will always feel guilty about Mom's death. To this day, I will never forgive myself for stopping for breakfast. I believe Mom's suicide was intended to be a cry for attention. I don't think Mom intended to die. If I had come straight home, I would have found Mom in time to revive her. Eleanor and the kids seemed oblivious to the sadness that hovered over the house now that Mom was gone. Only I seemed to feel the emptiness.

The Little Prick had been elected and instead of being the puppet Sammy had anticipated, Johnson began taking his new role seriously. He immediately started closing down Terre Haute, starting with me. Somewhere along the way, Johnson had started believing his own hype about being the reformer his campaign promised he would be.

It was definitely time to regroup, maybe start over. It wouldn't be the first time I've had to restart my life. If there is one thing I've learned it's that persistence is everything.

Anticipating a change in leadership, I had already begun working on a new business plan. I purchased a Tandy personal computer from Radio Shack two months ago which I used to track all the data from the insurance business. It took up a lot of room at the office, but looked very impressive. I was getting more proficient and had taught myself a little lynx programming along the way. All this was in preparation for my next business venture. I had reviewed my connections, and thought about how I could tap into those resources. I came up with an idea that could make me a great deal of money….and it was legit. I have to admit the idea of going legit was out of character for me, but I was getting older and didn't fancy always looking over my shoulder. It was a crossroads for me. I worked hard to make connections with all the right people, but those people were about to change. It seemed redundant to start all over with a new group.

As appointed positions, Sheriff Wesley and the Chief were waiting for their notices. "I'm too old to go back to being a beat cop," said the Chief. "The wife and I have already discussed it. We bought some property in Tennessee years ago, and we're going to build our retirement home. I'm actually getting excited about the prospect."

"What about you, Wesley," I asked. "What's your next move?"

"I've got two more years till retirement. I'm going to hold out. I'll be demoted to a desk captain, but I can handle that for two years," he said.

"What have you got planned, Don?" Stevens asked.

"I've been toying with an idea for several months. I'm opening Vigo Security Systems. I've checked out the equipment and installation requirements. Ron will be my installer, and I'll work directly with the customers. It's been a long time since I started a new venture, and I'm looking forward to it," I said.

"I've been offered a position at a law firm in Indianapolis. I'll specialize as their criminal trial lawyer, and I'm looking forward to being in a courtroom setting again. I start in a week. As soon as we can sell the house, Julia will be joining me," said Wiseman. "I'll be handling the high profile, criminal cases, and if all goes well, I should be a junior partner within the year." There was no doubt in my mind that Wiseman would make junior partner.

It was a bittersweet dinner. We all knew we would go our separate ways. We were comrades manipulating the system and syphoning as much money as possible for the last twenty years, but the great game was over. We ate and drank like soldiers coming home from their last successful campaign.

In the weeks that followed, Johnson surprised Sammy and everyone else by actually sticking with his reform platform. He closed the last eighteen "boarding houses" in the "red-light district", putting the working girls out on the streets. I had already shuttered the keno game after the raid at the reservation, so there was no publicity-making opportunity there. He did claim credit for putting enough heat on the games, that I voluntarily closed them. He was right. The Sheriff and the Chief were replaced with eager young men promising to work as a team with the judges to make Terre Haute a safe place to raise children. I should note that we never dealt in drugs or enticed children into any unwholesome activities. We were about making money from consenting adults, and I resented the notion that we conducted nefarious activities designed to corrupt our youth.

The Saturday Evening Post ran a special article detailing the "taking back of a small town by their people". Johnson was getting all the support and publicity he could handle. Chicago even gave up on incorporating Terre Haute into their sphere of influence. It proved to be a small town with too few resources to make it profitable. Terre Haute was again in the "hands of the people" as Johnson said. He actually believed his hype and became a true reformer.

I focused my energies on developing my fledgling company. Today I'm picking up the service truck from the graphic artist. I purchased a panel van and equipped it with the appropriate shelving and drawers to accommodate all the equipment necessary to install a security system. After everything was installed, I delivered the van to a graphic artist who was about to turn it into a moving billboard for the Vigo Security Systems. When I pulled into the parking lot, the van was sitting out front of the building on Wabash. He had done a wonderful job. It told the public everything we did without making the van so cluttered as to make it difficult to read as it passed. Vigo Security Systems was officially born.

Ron drove the van back to the office and I followed behind in the Caddy. The insurance and bail bond business had been relegated to one room of the house. The other three rooms had been dedicated to the new business. The Tandy computer, a desk and two chairs filled one room which served as the official office for Vigo Security Systems. One room stored the marketing and office supplies for all the businesses, and had a kitchenette on one wall. The third room housed the actual equipment; monitors, alarm boxes, and all the small parts necessary for installation. The space was tight, but I planned every inch of space so it functioned well. My police friends fed me leads of people who had been vandalized or robbed, for which they were paid a referral fee. The business flourished. It turns out that you CAN make as much money legally as you do illegally.

Mary and Sarah continued to live in Sarah's family home, and seemed quite content. Sarah even found a gentlemen to spend some time with. The police never solved Roy's murder, and eventually chalked it up to a mob hit. I decided not to share my theory of Roy's murder, but I was 99% sure Mary made the ultimate move to keep Sarah happy and safe. I miss Roy, but I have developed some new relationships with people I have met in the security business. My golf game is back on track, with new foursomes, but the flavor of the game is totally different. Roy and I had a connection that was unusual and I miss him. I will never have that kind of relationship again.

I tried to keep in touch with Tony, but after a few months I was told he moved to Mexico and they didn't know how to get in touch with him. I even flew to Vegas to talk with the staff. All those people who were so friendly when Tony and I made our rounds, suddenly couldn't remember anything about where he was or what he was doing in Mexico. I finally resigned myself to the fact that

Tony was probably safely buried in the Las Vegas desert.

And then there was Mom. I will **always** feel guilty about Mom's death. To this day, I will never forgive myself still have nightmares about that night. I sued Kroger for $100,000 for mishandling her arrest, and won. That did very little to ease the nightmares or the sense of loss with Mom's death. There's a hole in my heart.

The excitement of balancing all the necessary payoffs and personalities that kept the prior businesses afloat have been replaced with the challenge of keeping up with the technology necessary in the new business. Working the security business is almost like an enjoyable retirement. I still work too many hours, but the pressure is significantly less which is reflected in my lowered blood pressure. I sleep better and I find I'm drinking and smoking less. Fortunately, I'm also making a shit-load of money so I can still enjoy all the perks my prior illegal income provided.

I'm eager to play out this next chapter. You really can teach an old dog new tricks. . . . if he's willing, and I'm always willing.

Post Script

Dad continued to operate Vigo Security Systems quite successfully. Unfortunately, his hard living lifestyle, coupled with his penchant for self-adjusting his insulin, caused major health problems. He initially lost most of his eyesight. He could recognize people by their voice or the vague outline of their body, but he couldn't see much beyond that. Always the salesman, he was able to hide his disability from associates. He explained Ron's constant presence as an opportunity to teach him the finer points of running the business. Besides, "I've earned the right to be chauffeured around," as he liked to say.

He suffered an injury to his toe which never healed and eventually gangrene set in. He fought going to the hospital but ultimately had no choice. The surgeon who removed the offending leg, explained the gangrene had moved to his chest cavity and there was nothing that could be done. He lasted a week before his body gave up, and he never regained consciousness after the surgery.

Dad died at 62 years old. We played his anthem, 'My Way', by ole blue eyes at the funeral.

The End